It's another great book from CGP...

GCSE Additional Science is all about **understanding how science works**.
And not only that — understanding it well enough to be able to **question**
what you hear on TV and read in the papers.

But don't panic. This book includes all the **science facts** you need to learn,
and shows you how they work in the real world. It even includes
a **free** Online Edition you can read on your computer or tablet.

How to get your free Online Edition

Just go to **cgpbooks.co.uk/extras** and enter this code...

2193 5161 6267 0950

By the way, this code only works for one person. If somebody else has used
this book before you, they might have already claimed the Online Edition.

CGP — still the best! ☺

Our sole aim here at CGP is to produce the highest
quality books — carefully written, immaculately presented
and dangerously close to being funny.

Then we work our socks off to get them
out to you — at the cheapest possible prices.

Contents

Published by CGP

From original material by Richard Parsons.

Editors:
Katie Braid, Joe Brazier, Emma Elder, Ben Fletcher, Murray Hamilton, Edmund Robinson,
Helen Ronan, Lyn Setchell, Hayley Thompson, Julie Wakeling, Dawn Wright.

ISBN: 978 1 84762 747 6

With thanks to Charlotte Burrows, Janet Cruse-Sawyer, Philip Dobson, Ian Francis,
David Hickinson and Jane Towle for the proofreading.
With thanks to Jan Greenway, Laura Jakubowski and Laura Stoney for the copyright research.

Pages 37, 38, 90 and 92 contain public sector information published by the Health and Safety
Executive and licensed under the Open Government Licence v1.0.

Data used to construct table on page 91 from World Nuclear Association:
www.world-nuclear.org

Printed by Elanders Ltd, Newcastle upon Tyne.
Clipart from Corel®

The Scientific Process

This section isn't about how to 'do' science — but it does show you the way most scientists work, and how they try to find decent explanations for things that happen. It's pretty important stuff.

Scientists Come Up With Hypotheses...

1) Scientists try to explain things. Everything.

2) They start by observing (looking at) something they don't understand, e.g. an illness a person has.

3) They then try to come up with a hypothesis:

- A hypothesis ISN'T just a SUMMARY of their observations (e.g. bars of gold are very heavy).

- It's an EXPLANATION for them (e.g. bars of gold are very heavy because gold is very dense).

- Observations don't show what the hypothesis should be. In order to come up with a good hypothesis, scientists need to use their imagination.

- A good hypothesis should explain ALL of the observations made.

...and Then Test Them

1) The next step is to test whether the hypothesis might be right or not.

2) This involves making a prediction — a statement based on the hypothesis, which can be tested.

3) Predictions are tested by collecting evidence (i.e. data) from investigations.

4) If evidence from experiments backs up a prediction, people are more likely to believe that the hypothesis is true.

5) If the evidence doesn't fit with the hypothesis, then either those results or the hypothesis must be wrong.

6) Sometimes a hypothesis will explain all the data and still turn out to be wrong — that's why every hypothesis needs to be tested further (see next page).

Different Scientists Can Come Up With Different Explanations

1) Different scientists can make the same observations and come up with different explanations for them.

2) Sometimes a scientist's personal background will affect the way he or she thinks. E.g. a genetic scientist might lean towards a genetic explanation for a certain disease, but someone else might think it's more about the environment.

3) In these situations, it's important to test the explanations as much as possible — to see which one is most likely to be true.

Science is a "real-world" subject...

Science isn't just about explaining things that people want to find out about. If scientists can explain something that happens in the world, then maybe they can predict what will happen in the future. They might even be able to control future events. This could make life a bit better in some way, either for themselves or for other people.

The Scientific Process

The scientific process can be quite <u>long</u>... which is why there's another page on it.
I bet you just <u>can't wait</u> to see how it ends up. Enjoy.

Several Scientists <u>Will Test</u> a Hypothesis

1) Scientific explanations are <u>judged</u> by <u>other scientists</u>.
This is called the '<u>peer review</u>' process.

2) New scientific explanations are announced at
<u>scientific conferences</u> or in <u>peer-reviewed journals</u>.

A <u>peer-reviewed</u> journal is a science magazine where <u>other scientists</u> check scientific explanations <u>before</u> the journal is published.

3) Once other scientists have found out about a hypothesis,
they'll start to base their <u>own predictions</u> on it and carry out their
<u>own experiments</u>. This allows them to <u>test</u> the new hypothesis.

4) When other scientists test the new hypothesis they will also try
to <u>reproduce</u> the earlier results.

5) Results that <u>can't be reproduced</u> by another scientist <u>aren't</u> very <u>reliable</u>
(they're hard to trust). Scientists are usually very <u>doubtful</u> about them.

If <u>Evidence</u> Supports a Hypothesis, It's Accepted — for Now

1) If a hypothesis <u>survives</u> the peer review process, then scientists start to
have a lot of <u>confidence</u> in it and accept it as a <u>theory</u>.

2) Once scientists have gone through this process and accepted
a theory, they take a lot of <u>persuading</u> to <u>drop it</u>.

3) Until a <u>better explanation</u> is found, the <u>tried and tested</u> theory
is likely to <u>stick around</u>.

Some theories are 'models' — they show simply what
is going on with objects we can't see, e.g. the model
of the atom (see page 27). Other theories might
describe the link between different things using maths.

That's my theory and I'm sticking to it...

So there you have it. These two pages contain <u>everything you need to know</u> about how scientists make an
<u>observation</u>, then come up with a nice, neat <u>explanation</u> for it. And in case you were thinking this has nothing to
do with you, you'll need to know it for your <u>controlled assessment</u> (see pages 94-97) and for your <u>exams</u>.

Data

This page is all about what scientists do with <u>data</u> and why it's so <u>important</u>...

Scientists Need Reliable Data, Not Opinion, to Back Up an Explanation

1) The only <u>scientific</u> way to <u>test a hypothesis</u> is to collect <u>reliable data</u>.

2) Reliable data is data that has been <u>repeated</u> by a scientist lots of times or <u>reproduced</u> by other scientists in their own experiments.

3) <u>Opinions</u> aren't <u>reliable data</u> — they can't be <u>reproduced</u> in an experiment by other scientists.

Measurements Will Always Vary

1) If you take a lot of measurements of the <u>same thing</u>, you won't always get the <u>same result</u>.

2) This could be for lots of reasons, e.g. you made a <u>mistake</u> when measuring (<u>human error</u>).

3) Because measurements of the same thing always vary, you <u>can't be sure</u> that any <u>one measurement</u> will give you the <u>true value</u> of whatever it is you're measuring.

Repeating Measurements Helps You to Estimate the True Value

1) To get a <u>good estimate</u> of the true value, scientists must <u>repeat</u> their <u>measurements</u>.

2) Repeated measurements will have a <u>range</u> of values.
The <u>true value</u> should lie somewhere within this range.

3) The true value can be <u>estimated</u> by <u>calculating</u> the <u>mean</u> (average).
Just add up all the repeated results and divide by the total number of results.

4) Measurements that are obviously <u>outside</u> the range of repeated results are called <u>outliers</u>.

5) Outliers are usually a sign that something has gone <u>wrong</u>.

6) If possible, a scientist will <u>check</u> the measurement — if they can work out what went wrong, they'll <u>ignore</u> it.

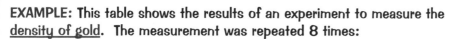

EXAMPLE: This table shows the results of an experiment to measure the <u>density of gold</u>. The measurement was repeated 8 times:

1) The result of <u>test 3</u> is very <u>different</u> from the others. It's an <u>outlier</u>.

2) Most of the measurements lie in the <u>range</u> of 19.1 – 19.5 g/cm³.

3) So the <u>true value</u> of the density of gold should be between 19.1 and 19.5 g/cm³.

4) A <u>mean</u> (average) gives you the <u>best estimate</u> of the <u>true</u> value. In this case it's <u>19.3 g/cm³</u> (the <u>outlier</u> was <u>ignored</u>).

Test	Density of gold (g/cm³)
1	19.3
2	19.4
3	12.8
4	19.1
5	19.3
6	19.2
7	19.5
8	19.2

Working out averages — it's just mean...

Data is used to test <u>every</u> hypothesis, so it really is <u>pretty blummin' important</u>. What a shame then, that estimating the <u>true value</u> and spotting <u>outliers</u> isn't just a bit more fun... sigh...

Correlation and Cause

Correlation and cause come up a lot in science, so it's important that you understand the difference.

A Correlation is a Relationship Between Two Factors

1) Scientists think about scientific processes as a load of different factors which might affect an outcome. For example, if the outcome is winning a motor race, it might be affected by factors such as drag, the mass of the car and the driving force of the engine.

2) They collect data and use it to look for relationships between a factor and an outcome.

3) If an outcome happens when a factor is there, but not when it isn't there, scientists say there's a correlation.

4) If an outcome increases or decreases as a factor increases or decreases, they're also said to be correlated.

A Correlation Doesn't Prove One Thing Causes Another

1) Just because there's a correlation between a factor and an outcome, it doesn't mean that the factor causes the outcome.

2) There might be another, hidden factor that's affecting them both. Here's an example:

> 1) Primary school children with bigger feet tend to be better at maths.
> There's a correlation between the factor (big feet) and the outcome (better maths skills).
> 2) But it'd be crazy to say that having big feet causes you to be better at maths.
> 3) There's another (hidden) factor involved — their age.
> 4) Older children are usually better at maths. They also usually have bigger feet.

3) Sometimes a correlation is when a factor makes an outcome more likely, but not certain. E.g. if you eat a diet high in saturated fat, it increases your risk of heart disease, but doesn't mean you will get it.

Scientists Need to Do Fair Tests

1) To check whether a factor causes an outcome, a scientist must do a scientific study.

2) To make their study a fair test, the scientist must control all the other factors that might affect the outcome. This will make sure that the only factor affecting the outcome is the one being studied (see page 94).

3) In a study, scientists can't usually test the whole population (e.g. all the organisms of a species) so they compare samples instead. A sample is just a small group from the population.

4) There are two ways that scientists can make sure their study is a fair test when comparing samples:

- The samples can be the same in every way — apart from the factor that they're investigating.
- The samples can be chosen at random. Then it's equally likely that all samples will be affected by other factors in the same way.

5) The larger the sample size used in a study, the more confident a scientist can be about their hypothesis.

All sheep die — Elvis died, so he must have been a sheep...

You hear about correlations on the news all the time. Reporters often make the mistake of thinking that if two things are correlated then one must cause the other. However, you can't, can't, can't just think this. Got that?

Science — Benefits, Costs, Risks and Ethics

Science can give us amazing things — cures for diseases, space travel, heated toilet seats...
But sometimes, these things come at a cost.

Scientific Technology Usually Has Benefits and Costs

1) Scientists have created loads of new technologies that could improve our lives.
2) But some new technologies can have unintended impacts (things we didn't mean to happen).
3) They can also have undesired impacts (things we didn't want to happen).
4) These impacts can have a negative effect on our quality of life or the environment.

Nothing is Completely Risk-Free

1) Everything that you do has a risk attached to it.
2) New technology can bring new risks, e.g. some scientists think using a mobile phone a lot may be harmful.
3) You can estimate the size of a risk based on how many times something has happened in a big sample (e.g. 100 000 people) over a set amount of time (say, a year).
4) To make a decision about an activity that involves a risk, we need to think about:

   • the chance of the risk happening,
   • how serious the consequences (results) would be if it did.

5) So if an activity involves a risk that's very likely to happen, with serious consequences if it does, that activity is considered high risk.
6) Most people are happier to accept a risk if the consequences don't last long and aren't serious.
7) People also tend to be more willing to accept a risk if they're choosing to do something (e.g. go scuba diving).
8) They're less willing to accept a risk if the risk is forced on them (e.g. having a nuclear power station built next door).

There are risks involved in building a nuclear power station.

Some Questions Can't be Answered by Science

1) Science can often raise important issues to do with ethics — whether it's right or wrong to do something.
2) The question of whether something is ethically right or wrong can't ever be answered by experiments.
3) That's because there is no "right" or "wrong" answer.
4) The best we can do is make a decision that most people are more or less happy to live by.

There Are Two Key Arguments About Ethical Dilemmas

1
• Some people think that certain actions are always unnatural or wrong.
• This means that, whatever the benefits, they feel these actions are unacceptable.

2
Some people may say that the right decision is the one that brings the greatest benefit to the greatest number of people.

Hmmm, tricky...

As you can see, science isn't just about knowing your facts. You need to think about the issues involved in new technology — as well as the kinds of arguments people consider to make decisions about what should be done.

Cell Structure and Function

Lots of important chemical reactions happen in cells — you need to know about the different parts involved.

Plant and Animal Cells Have Similarities and Differences

Most animal and plant cells have the following parts — make sure you know them all:

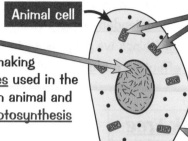

Nucleus

1) It contains DNA (see page 15).
2) DNA contains the instructions for making proteins. For example, the enzymes used in the chemical reactions of respiration (in animal and plant cells, see pages 8-9) and photosynthesis (in plant cells only, see page 10).

Mitochondria

These are where the enzymes needed for the reactions of aerobic respiration (see page 8) are found. It's also where the reactions take place.

Cell membrane

1) It holds the cell together.
2) It controls what goes in and out. For example, it lets gases and water pass through freely while acting as a barrier to other chemicals.

Cytoplasm

1) It's where proteins like enzymes (see page 7) are made.
2) Some enzyme-controlled reactions take place in the cytoplasm. For example, the reactions of anaerobic respiration (see page 9).

Plant cells also have a few extra things that animal cells don't have:

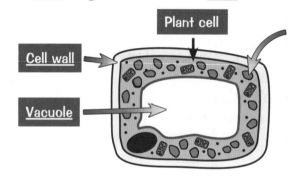

Chloroplasts

1) These are where the reactions for photosynthesis take place.
2) They contain a green substance called chlorophyll.
3) They also contain the enzymes needed for photosynthesis.

Yeast are Microorganisms

You need to learn the different parts of a yeast cell: ➡

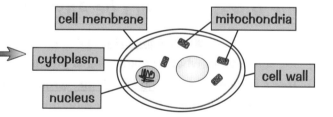

Bacteria Have a Simple Cell Structure

1) You need to know the different parts of a bacterial cell:
2) They don't have a nucleus. They have a circular molecule of DNA which floats around in the cytoplasm.
3) They don't have mitochondria either.

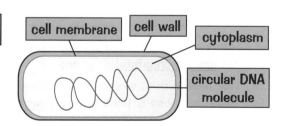

At yeast it's an easy page...

A simple way of learning this stuff is to copy it out into a table. Plus, it's good clean fun for all the family. Yay.

Enzymes

Without enzymes, all the <u>chemical reactions</u> taking place inside cells would run dead slowly — so your body wouldn't function properly. But enzymes won't work if they don't have the <u>right conditions</u>.

Enzymes *are* Proteins *Produced by* Living Things

> <u>ENZYMES</u> are proteins that <u>SPEED UP CHEMICAL REACTIONS</u>

The <u>instructions</u> for making enzymes and other proteins are found in a cell's <u>genes</u> (see page 15).

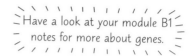
Have a look at your module B1 notes for more about genes.

Enzymes *are Very Specific*

1) <u>Chemical reactions</u> usually involve things either being <u>split apart</u> or <u>joined together</u>.
2) A <u>substrate</u> is a molecule that is <u>changed</u> in a reaction.
3) <u>Every</u> enzyme molecule has an <u>active site</u> — the part where a substrate <u>joins on</u> to the enzyme.
4) Enzymes are really <u>picky</u> — they usually only speed up <u>one reaction</u>.
5) This is because a substrate has to be the <u>correct shape</u> to <u>fit</u> into the <u>active site</u>.
6) This is called the <u>'lock and key' model</u>, because the substrate fits into the enzyme just like a key fits into a lock.

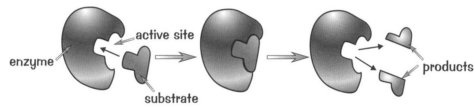

active site
enzyme
substrate
products

Enzymes *Need the Right Temperature and pH*

1) Enzymes need to be at a <u>specific temperature</u> to work at their <u>optimum</u> (when they're <u>most active</u>).
2) But, if it gets <u>too hot</u> the enzyme <u>won't work</u> any more.

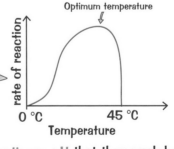

Optimum temperature

rate of reaction

0 °C   45 °C
Temperature

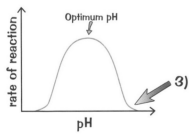

Optimum pH

rate of reaction

pH

3) All enzymes also have an <u>optimum pH</u> that they work best at.

If only enzymes could speed up revision...

Just like you've got to have the correct key for a lock, enzymes have got to have the <u>right substrate</u>. If a substrate <u>doesn't fit</u>, the enzyme <u>won't</u> speed up the reaction...

Aerobic Respiration

Respiration doesn't sound very rock 'n' roll but it keeps you alive. The basic processes of life (e.g. movement) depend on chemical reactions. Most of these reactions are powered by the energy released by respiration.

Respiration is NOT "Breathing In and Out"

1) Respiration is NOT breathing in and breathing out, as you might think.

Food molecules are things like glucose (a sugar).

> RESPIRATION is a series of chemical reactions that RELEASE ENERGY by breaking down large FOOD MOLECULES. It happens in EVERY LIVING CELL.

2) The energy released by respiration is used to power some of the chemical reactions that happen in cells, e.g. the reactions involved in:

MOVEMENT

Energy is needed to make muscles contract.

MAKING LARGE MOLECULES

Energy is needed to join molecules together. Lots of large molecules (polymers) are made by joining smaller molecules together. For example:
- Glucose is joined together to make things like starch and cellulose in plant cells.
- Glucose and nitrogen are joined together to make amino acids.
  Amino acids are joined together to make proteins.
  This happens in plant cells, animal cells and microorganisms.

3) There are two types of respiration — aerobic and anaerobic.

Aerobic Respiration Needs Plenty of Oxygen

1) Aerobic respiration takes place in animal and plant cells, and in some microorganisms.

2) It releases more energy per glucose molecule than anaerobic respiration.

Anaerobic respiration is covered on the next page.

3) You need to learn the word equation of aerobic respiration:

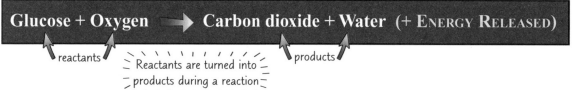

Glucose + Oxygen ➡ Carbon dioxide + Water (+ ENERGY RELEASED)

reactants *Reactants are turned into products during a reaction* *products*

Don't stop respirin' — hold on to that feelin' (of being alive)...

Isn't it strange to think that each individual living cell in your body is respiring every second of every day, releasing energy from the food you eat. Next time someone accuses you of being lazy you could claim that you're busy respiring — it's enough to make anyone feel tired.

Anaerobic Respiration

If you thought that was it for respiration, you'd be wrong. Next up, anaerobic respiration...

Anaerobic Respiration *Doesn't Use Oxygen*

1) Anaerobic respiration takes place in animal and plant cells and some microorganisms.

2) It happens when there's very little or no oxygen. For example:

- Plant root cells respire anaerobically in soil that's soaked with water (waterlogged).
- Human muscle cells respire anaerobically during vigorous (intense) exercise.
- Bacteria can get under your skin through puncture wounds caused by things like nails. Only bacteria that can respire anaerobically can survive there.

Anaerobic Respiration *Can Produce Lactic Acid*

In animal cells and some bacteria anaerobic respiration produces lactic acid:

Glucose ➡ Lactic Acid (+ ENERGY RELEASED)

reactant   product

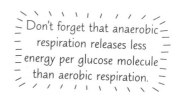
Don't forget that anaerobic respiration releases less energy per glucose molecule than aerobic respiration.

Anaerobic Respiration *Can Also Produce Ethanol and Carbon Dioxide*

1) In plant cells and some microorganisms (like yeast), anaerobic respiration produces ethanol and carbon dioxide:

Glucose ➡ Ethanol + Carbon Dioxide (+ ENERGY RELEASED)

reactant   products

2) Fermentation is when microorganisms break down sugars into other products as they respire anaerobically. Humans use fermentation to make lots of things, for example:

BIOGAS
1) Lots of different microorganisms are used to produce biogas (a fuel).
2) They ferment plant and animal waste, which contains carbohydrates.

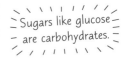
Sugars like glucose are carbohydrates.

BREAD
1) Yeast ferment the carbohydrates in flour.
2) This releases carbon dioxide and causes bread to rise.

ALCOHOL
Yeast ferment sugar to form alcohol (ethanol).

Anaerobic respiration — the best thing since sliced bread...

Anaerobic respiration is way more useful than it sounds — it's given us bread, and so more importantly, the wonder of toast. The world would be a very sad place without toast — there'd be nothing to put your beans on...

Photosynthesis

Some organisms <u>make</u> their <u>own food</u>. It's not restaurant-quality grub, but you need to know <u>how</u> it's done.

Photosynthesis *Produces Glucose*

<u>PHOTOSYNTHESIS</u> is a series of chemical reactions that <u>USES ENERGY</u> from <u>SUNLIGHT</u> to <u>PRODUCE FOOD</u>.

1) The 'food' it produces is <u>glucose</u> — a <u>sugar</u>.
2) Photosynthesis happens in:
   - The <u>cells</u> in <u>green parts</u> of <u>plants</u>, e.g. leaf cells.
   - Some microorganisms, e.g. <u>phytoplankton</u>.
3) <u>Chlorophyll</u> is needed for photosynthesis to happen.
4) It's a <u>green substance</u> which captures <u>sunlight</u> energy.
   The energy is used to convert <u>carbon dioxide</u> (CO_2) and <u>water</u> into <u>glucose</u>.
5) <u>Oxygen</u> is produced as a <u>waste product</u> of photosynthesis. Here's the equation:

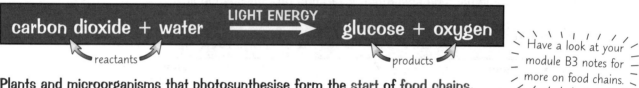

$$\text{carbon dioxide} + \text{water} \xrightarrow{\text{LIGHT ENERGY}} \text{glucose} + \text{oxygen}$$

reactants   products

Have a look at your module B3 notes for more on food chains.

6) Plants and microorganisms that photosynthesise form the <u>start</u> of <u>food chains</u>.
   - They make the <u>energy</u> from the Sun <u>available</u> to other organisms.
   - They do this by <u>changing</u> it into <u>glucose</u>.
   - The energy is <u>passed on</u> to other organisms when the plants and microorganisms are <u>eaten</u>.

Plants Use the Glucose *in Three Main Ways*

(1) *Glucose is Used for* Respiration

1) Plants use some of the glucose for <u>respiration</u> (see page 8).
2) This process <u>releases energy</u> from the glucose.

(2) *Glucose is Used to Make Chemicals for Growth*

1) Glucose is converted into <u>cellulose</u>.
2) Glucose is combined with <u>nitrogen</u> to make <u>amino acids</u>.
   The <u>nitrogen</u> comes <u>from nitrates</u> taken up from the <u>soil</u> by plant roots.
   Amino acids are joined together to make <u>proteins</u>.
3) Glucose is also used to help make <u>chlorophyll</u>.

(3) *Glucose is Stored as Starch*

<u>Glucose</u> is turned into <u>starch</u> and <u>stored</u> in roots, stems and leaves.

Convert this page into stored information...

Without plants we'd all be pretty stuffed really — plants are able to use the Sun's energy to <u>make glucose</u>.
This is the <u>energy source</u> which humans and all other animals need for <u>respiration</u> (see page 8).

Rate of Photosynthesis

The rate of photosynthesis is affected by environmental conditions...

Three Factors **Affect the Rate of Photosynthesis**

1)   There are three factors that can affect the rate of photosynthesis...

> 1)   amount of <u>light</u>

> 2)   amount of CO_2 3)   <u>temperature</u>

2)   Any of these three factors can become the <u>limiting factor</u>.

3)   This just means that it <u>stops</u> photosynthesis from <u>happening any faster</u>.

1) Not Enough Light Slows Down the Rate of Photosynthesis

1)   Light provides the <u>energy</u> needed for photosynthesis.

2)   As the <u>light level</u> is raised, the rate of photosynthesis <u>increases steadily</u> — but only up to a <u>certain point</u>.

3)   Beyond that, it <u>won't</u> make any difference. By then it'll be either the <u>temperature</u> or the <u>CO_2 level</u> which is the limiting factor.

2) Too Little Carbon Dioxide Also Slows It Down

1)   As with light level, the amount of <u>CO_2</u> will only increase the rate of photosynthesis up to a point.

2)   As long there's loads of <u>light</u> and <u>CO_2</u> then the factor limiting photosynthesis must be <u>temperature</u>.

3) The Temperature Has to be Just Right

1)   The <u>enzymes</u> (see page 7) needed for photosynthesis work more <u>slowly</u> at <u>low temperatures</u>.

2)   But if the plant gets <u>too hot</u>, the enzymes it needs for photosynthesis and its other reactions will <u>stop working</u>.

Don't blame it on the sunshine, don't blame it on the CO_2...

...don't blame it on the temperature, blame it on the plant. You might get asked to <u>use (interpret) data</u> on factors that <u>limit</u> the <u>rate of photosynthesis</u> in the exam, so get the info on this page burned into your brain.

Investigating Photosynthesis

You need to know about how to <u>investigate</u> (look into) the <u>effect of light</u> on <u>plants</u>.

You Need to Know How to Take a Transect

1) <u>Transects</u> are a way of <u>investigating</u> how something <u>changes across an area</u>.
2) To <u>set up</u> a transect you just run a <u>tape measure</u> between <u>two fixed points</u>.
3) Then all you do is <u>start</u> at <u>one end</u> of the transect and <u>collect</u> the <u>data</u> you want.
4) Then <u>move</u> along the transect and <u>collect</u> the <u>data</u> again.
5) You just <u>keep collecting</u> data and <u>moving</u> until you reach the <u>end</u> of the transect.
6) For example, you could see how <u>light affects</u> where <u>plant species</u> are found (<u>distributed</u>) in an area. You could take a transect across an area where the <u>light level changes</u> (e.g. from woodland into an open field).

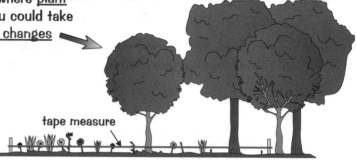

tape measure

You Need to Know About Some Things That'll Help You Collect Data

You need to know about a few other things that are <u>pretty useful</u> for investigating the effect of light on plants:

LIGHT METER

1) You'd need to <u>measure</u> the <u>level of light</u>, e.g. if you were comparing plants in areas with different levels of light.
2) You could use a <u>LIGHT METER</u> to do this. It's a <u>sensor</u> that <u>accurately</u> measures light level.

QUADRAT

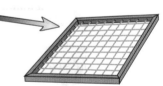

1) A quadrat is a <u>square frame</u> divided into a <u>grid</u> of 100 smaller squares.
2) You can see <u>how much</u> of the ground is <u>covered</u> by a plant species using a quadrat. You <u>count</u> how much of the <u>quadrat</u> is <u>covered</u> by the species. This will give you the <u>percentage cover</u> of the species.

IDENTIFICATION KEY

1) To find out what plant species you're looking at you could use an <u>IDENTIFICATION KEY</u>.
2) It's a <u>bunch of questions</u> that you can use to figure out what a plant is.
3) You start at question 1 and the answer is used to <u>narrow down</u> your options of what the plant could be.
4) As you answer more and more questions you're eventually just <u>left with one</u> possible species your plant could be.

Q1	Does it have a flower with white petals?	Yes	It's a daisy.
		No	Go to Q2
Q2	Is it long, green and thin?	Yes	It's grass.
		No	Go to Q3
Q3	Is it brown and sticky?	Yes	It's a stick.
		No	Your guess is as good as mine...

Is it never-ending and the least fun ever? Yes — it's revising for exams...

I think you'll agree that this has been the <u>most exciting</u> page in the book so far... Luckily this stuff is <u>pretty straightforward</u> — just learn the page until all this information has lodged itself in your brain box.

Diffusion and Osmosis

Some particles have their own special ways of moving in and out of cells...

Diffusion — Don't be Put Off by the Fancy Word

1) "Diffusion" is the steady movement of particles from places where there are lots of them to places where there are fewer of them.

2) That's all it is — particles just wanting to spread out.

3) Unfortunately you also have to learn the fancy way of saying the same thing, which is this:

> **DIFFUSION is the _passive overall movement_ of _particles_ from a region of their _HIGHER CONCENTRATION_ to a region of their _LOWER CONCENTRATION_.**

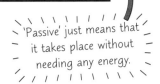
'Passive' just means that it takes place without needing any energy.

4) Here's an example — when plants photosynthesise they use up CO_2 and produce O_2 (see page 10). These gases pass in and out of plant leaves by diffusion.

Osmosis is a Specific Case of Diffusion, That's All

1) Osmosis is a type of diffusion.

2) It's the passive movement of water molecules from an area of higher concentration to an area of lower concentration.

> **Osmosis is the overall _movement of water_ from a _DILUTE_ to a _MORE CONCENTRATED_ solution through a _partially permeable membrane_.**

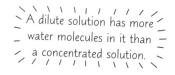
A dilute solution has more water molecules in it than a concentrated solution.

3) A partially permeable membrane is just one that only allows certain substances to diffuse through it. For example, it may only allow small molecules like water to pass through and not larger molecules like sucrose.

4) This concentrated sucrose solution gets more dilute as more water moves in. The water acts like it's trying to even up the concentration either side of the membrane.

5) Plants take in water by osmosis. There's usually a higher concentration of water in the soil than there is inside the plant. The water is drawn into the root by osmosis.

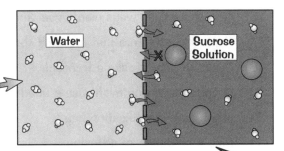

Water | Sucrose Solution

Net movement of water molecules

Revision by diffusion — you wish...

Wouldn't that be great — if all the ideas in this book would just steadily drift across into your mind, from an area of high concentration (in the book) to an area of low concentration (in your mind — no offence). Actually, that will probably happen if you read it again. Why don't you give it a go...

Revision Summary for Module B4

Now it's time to find out if you know your stuff. Have a bash at the questions, go back and check anything you're not sure about, then try again. Practise until you can answer all these questions really easily without having to look back at the section. I know you want to look at the section again, right now, as it is so exciting and so beautifully made. But you can't — not until you've had a go at these equally thrilling questions...

1) What is the function (job) of:
   a) the nucleus
   b) mitochondria
   c) the cell membrane
   d) the cytoplasm

2) Name three things that plant cells have and animal cells don't.

3) Yeast cells have mitochondria and a nucleus. True or false?

4) What type of cells have a cell wall but no nucleus?

5) Give a definition of an enzyme.

6) Describe the 'lock and key' model.

7) Name two things that affect how quickly an enzyme works.

8) Name two things that the energy released by respiration is used for.

9) What type of respiration, aerobic or anaerobic, releases more energy per glucose molecule?

10) Write the word equation for aerobic respiration.

11) Give an example of when human cells respire anaerobically.

12) Anaerobic respiration releases energy. What else does it produce in:
    a) animal cells
    b) yeast cells

13) Briefly describe how bread is made using yeast.

14) What happens during photosynthesis?

15) Write the word equation for photosynthesis.

16) Give three main ways plants use glucose.

17) Name three factors that can limit the rate of photosynthesis.

18) Describe how to take a transect.

19) Describe how you might use a quadrat when investigating plants.

20) What is an identification key?

21) Give a definition of diffusion.

22) Give two examples of chemicals that can move in or out of leaf cells by diffusion.

23) What is osmosis?

DNA — Making Proteins

All the instructions for how to grow and develop are contained in your <u>DNA</u>. DNA molecules are basically a long list of <u>instructions</u> for how to make <u>all the proteins</u> in your body.

DNA *is a* Double Helix *of* Paired Bases

1) A DNA molecule has <u>two strands</u> coiled together.

2) It's in the shape of a <u>double helix</u> (two spirals).

3) DNA has just <u>four</u> different bases — A, C, G and T.

4) The two strands are <u>held together</u> by the <u>bases pairing up</u>. The bases always pair up in the same way — A-T and C-G. This is called <u>base pairing</u>.

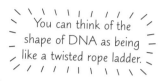

You can think of the shape of DNA as being like a twisted rope ladder.

base on one strand is joined to a base on the other strand

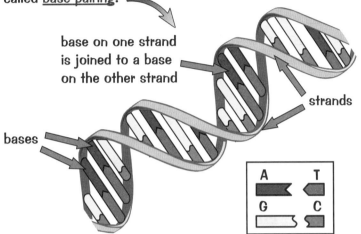

strands

bases

DNA *Controls the* Production *of* Proteins *in a* Cell

1) A <u>gene</u> is a <u>section of DNA</u>.

2) It contains the <u>code</u> (instructions) for making <u>one protein</u>.

3) It's the order of the <u>bases</u> in a gene that <u>tells the cell</u> how to make a <u>protein</u>.

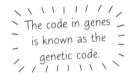

The code in genes is known as the genetic code.

Proteins *are* Made *in the* Cytoplasm

1) Proteins are made in the cell <u>cytoplasm</u> (see page 6).

2) DNA is found in the cell <u>nucleus</u>.

3) A <u>copy</u> of the DNA is made to get the information from the DNA to the cytoplasm.

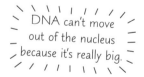

DNA can't move out of the nucleus because it's really big.

What do DNA and a game of rounders have in common?

...they both have four bases. Genes <u>control</u> what <u>proteins</u> are made. And proteins are essential things — all your body's enzymes are proteins and enzymes control the making of your other, non-protein bits.

Cell Division — Mitosis and Meiosis

There are <u>two</u> ways that your body makes <u>new cells</u> — you need to know about both of them.

New Cells are Needed for Growth and Repair

The cells of your body <u>divide</u> in two to <u>produce more cells</u>. This is so your body can <u>grow</u> and <u>replace</u> damaged cells. Cells <u>grow</u> and <u>divide</u> over and over again — this is called the <u>cell cycle</u>. There are two stages...

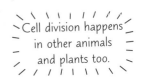
Cell division happens in other animals and plants too.

First the cell grows in size and copies its contents...

1) The cell has to <u>copy everything</u> it contains. This is so that when it <u>splits</u> in half the two new cells will contain the right amount of material.

2) The <u>number</u> of <u>organelles</u> (cell parts) <u>increases</u> during cell growth.

3) The <u>chromosomes</u> are <u>copied</u>, so that the cell has <u>two copies</u> of its DNA:

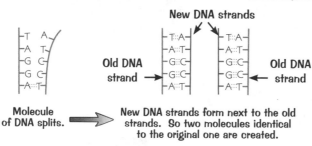

New DNA strands

Old DNA strand →

Old DNA ← strand

Molecule of DNA splits. → New DNA strands form next to the old strands. So two molecules identical to the original one are created.

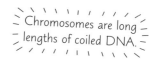
Chromosomes are long lengths of coiled DNA.

...then it splits into two by Mitosis

1) The chromosomes <u>line up</u> at the centre of the cell. They're pulled apart to <u>opposite ends</u> of the cell.

2) <u>Membranes</u> form around each of the sets of chromosomes. These become the <u>nuclei</u> of the two new cells.

3) Then the <u>cytoplasm</u> divides.

4) You now have <u>two new cells</u> with exactly the same DNA. They're <u>genetically identical</u> to <u>each other</u> and to the <u>parent</u> (original) <u>cell</u>.

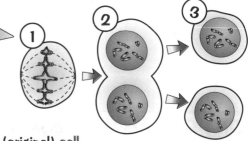

Gametes are Produced by Meiosis

1) All the cells in your body divide by mitosis <u>except</u> cells in your reproductive organs.

2) They divide by <u>meiosis</u> to form sperm or egg cells (<u>gametes</u>).

Gametes Have Half the Usual Number of Chromosomes

1) During <u>sexual reproduction</u>, an egg and a sperm combine.

2) This forms a new cell, called a <u>zygote</u>.

3) All human body cells have <u>two copies</u> of each chromosome.

4) But gametes only have <u>one copy</u> of each chromosome.

5) So when the egg and sperm combine the zygote will contain <u>two copies</u> of each chromosome — one <u>set</u> from <u>each parent</u>.

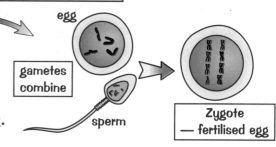

egg

gametes combine

sperm

Zygote — fertilised egg

A cell's favourite computer game — divide and conquer...

No matter how bad <u>cell division</u> looks, it could be worse — you could be in maths, <u>dividing massive numbers</u>...

Animal Development

Every living organism is made up of cells. Multicellular organisms are organisms that have lots of cells.
Most of their cells are specialised to do a particular job, e.g. carry oxygen around the body.

Cells in an Early Embryo Can Turn into Any Type of Cell

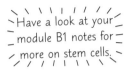
Have a look at your
module B1 notes for
more on stem cells.

1) A fertilised egg (zygote) divides by mitosis to produce an embryo.

2) To start with, the cells in the embryo are all the same (they're unspecialised).
    They're called embryonic stem cells.

3) Embryonic stem cells can divide to produce any type of specialised cell (e.g. blood cells, nerve cells).

4) In humans, all the cells in the embryo are unspecialised up to the eight cell stage.

5) After the eight cell stage, most of the stem cells in a human embryo start to specialise.

6) The embryo then begins to develop tissues and organs.

7) Tissues are groups of specialised cells. Organs are groups of specialised tissues.

8) Adult humans only have stem cells in certain places like the bone marrow.

9) Adult stem cells only turn into certain types of specialised cells.

eight cell
stage embryo

Different Cells Have Different Genes Switched On

Body cells are all the cells that make
you up, except sperm or egg cells.

1) All body cells contain the same genes.

2) However, in specialised cells most of the genes are not active
    (they're switched off).

3) This means they only produce the specific proteins they need.

4) Stem cells can switch on any gene during their development.

5) The genes that are active decide what type of cell a stem cell specialises into.

Stem Cells May be Able to Cure Many Diseases

ADULT STEM CELLS

1) Adult stem cells are already used to cure disease.

2) For example, people with some blood diseases (e.g. sickle-cell anaemia) can be treated
    by bone marrow transplants. Bone marrow is found in the middle of your bones.
    It contains stem cells that can turn into new blood cells.

EMBRYONIC STEM CELLS

1) Embryonic stem cells can be taken from very early human embryos.

2) These could be turned into specialised cells to replace faulty cells in sick people.

3) But some people think it's unethical (not right) to use embryonic stem cells. This is because
    the embryos that the stem cells come from are destroyed. The embryos could have become a person.

4) It's such a tricky issue that scientific research using embryonic stem cells is regulated
    (controlled) by the government.

Develop — birds do it, bees do it, even educated fleas do it...

Stem cell research is a sensitive issue, but you need to know what stem cells are and what they could be used
for. Not just to impress your friends, but because it might come up in your exam too. So learn this page.

Plant Development and Phototropism

Now you know all about animal development, it's time to learn about how plants develop and grow.

Meristems Contain Plant Stem Cells

1) In plants, the only cells that divide by mitosis are found in plant tissues called meristems.
2) Meristem tissue is found in the areas of a plant that are growing, e.g. the roots and shoots.
3) Meristems produce unspecialised cells. These cells can divide and form any cell type in the plant.
4) The unspecialised cells can become specialised and form tissues. For example, xylem and phloem (the water and food transport tissues).
5) These tissues can group together to form organs like leaves, roots, stems and flowers.

Clones of Plants Can be Produced from Cuttings

1) A cutting is part of a plant that has been cut off it.
2) Cuttings taken from an area of the plant that's growing will contain unspecialised meristem cells.
3) This means a whole new plant can grow from the cutting.
4) The new plant will be an identical copy (a clone) of the parent plant.
5) Gardeners often take cuttings from parent plants with desirable features, e.g. a nice flower colour. They plant cuttings to make identical copies of the parent plant.
6) To help cuttings to grow in soil you can add rooting powder.
   • Rooting powder contains plant hormones.
   • The hormones make the cuttings produce roots rapidly and start growing as new plants.

Phototropism is Growth Towards or Away From Light

1) Some parts of a plant, e.g. roots and shoots, can respond to light by growing in a certain direction. This is called phototropism.
2) Shoots are positively phototropic — they grow towards light.
3) Roots are negatively phototropic — they grow away from light.
4) Phototropism helps plants to survive:

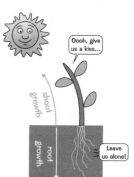

Oooh, give us a kiss...

shoot growth

root growth

Leave us alone!

Positive Phototropism

• Plants need sunlight for photosynthesis (see page 10).
• Without sunlight, plants can't photosynthesise. This means they don't produce the food they need for energy and growth.
• Photosynthesis occurs mainly in the leaves.
• This means it's important for plant shoots, which will grow leaves, to grow towards light.

Negative Phototropism

• Plants need nutrients and water from the soil to grow.
• Phototropism means roots grow away from light, down into the soil.
• This means they can absorb the water and nutrients the plant needs for healthy growth.

Cheery cells those Merry-stems...

After that thrilling page on plants I reckon you deserve a treat. So one delicious revision summary coming up...

Revision Summary for Module B5

Well done — you've finished another module. And what an incredibly tricky module it was — especially all the ins and outs of mitosis and meiosis. Award yourself a gold star and take a leisurely glance through these beautiful revision summary questions. Once you've glanced through them, you'll have to answer them. And then you'll have to check your answers and go back and revise any bits you got wrong. And then do the questions again. In fact, it's not really a matter of relaxing at all. More a matter of knuckling down to lots of hard work. Oops. Sorry.

1) How many different bases does DNA have?

2) Which bases always pair together?

3) What is a gene?

4) What are proteins made of?

5) Why is the order of bases in a gene important for making a protein?

6) Where in the cell are proteins made?

7) Where in the cell is DNA found?

8) During cell growth does the number of chromosomes double or halve?

9)* The table below compares mitosis and meiosis. Complete the table using crosses (X) and ticks (✓) to show whether the statements are true for mitosis or meiosis. The first row's been filled in for you.

	Mitosis	Meiosis
Its purpose is to provide new cells for growth and repair.	✓	X
Its purpose is to create gametes (sex cells).		
The cells produced are genetically identical.		
The cells produced contain half the number of chromosomes that were in the parent cell.		

10) What is the name of the cell produced when two gametes combine?

11) In a human embryo, all the cells are unspecialised until what stage?

12) How are the stem cells in an embryo different from the stem cells in an adult?

13) What determines the type of cell a stem cell becomes?

14) What name is given to the parts of plants where cells which divide by mitosis are found?

15) Name two types of tissue that the unspecialised cells in plants can turn into.

16) What is a cutting?

17) What do cuttings grow into?

18) Why do people like gardeners take cuttings?

19) What can be added to soil to encourage cuttings to grow roots?

20) What is phototropism?

21) Are shoots negatively or positively phototropic?

* Answers on page 100.

Module B5 — Growth and Development

The Nervous System

The environment around you <u>changes lots</u>. A <u>change</u> in the <u>environment</u> of an organism is called a <u>stimulus</u>. Organisms need to <u>respond to stimuli</u> in order to <u>survive</u>. This is where the <u>nervous system</u> steps in...

Multicellular Organisms **Need** Communication Systems

1) <u>Single celled</u> organisms can just <u>respond</u> to their environment.

2) But the cells of <u>multicellular</u> organisms need to <u>work together</u> so the <u>organism</u> can <u>respond</u> to stimuli.

3) So as multicellular organisms evolved they developed <u>nervous</u> and <u>hormonal communication systems</u>.

Multicellular organisms have lots of cells.

The Nervous System Detects **and Reacts** to Stimuli

Receptors

These are the cells that <u>detect stimuli</u>. Receptors are found in places like the <u>ears</u>, <u>eyes</u> and <u>skin</u>.

Sensory Neurones

The <u>neurones</u> that carry impulses (messages) from the <u>receptors</u> to the CNS.

Neurone is just a fancy word for 'nerve cell'. There's more on neurones on page 21.

Central Nervous System (CNS)

1) In <u>vertebrates</u> (animals with backbones) this is made up of the <u>brain</u> and <u>spinal cord</u> only.

2) In <u>mammals</u>, the CNS is connected to the rest of the body by <u>sensory neurones</u> and <u>motor neurones</u>. These neurones make up the <u>peripheral nervous system (PNS)</u>.

The next page tells you how all these parts work together to react to stimuli.

Motor Neurones

The <u>neurones</u> that carry impulses from the CNS to <u>effectors</u>.

Effectors

All your <u>muscles</u> and <u>glands</u>, which <u>respond</u> to <u>nervous impulses</u>.

Receptors **and** Effectors **can form part of Complex Organs**

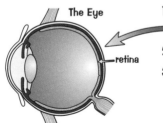

The Eye

retina

1) Receptors can form part of <u>larger</u>, <u>complex organs</u>, e.g. the <u>retina</u> of the <u>eye</u> is covered in <u>light receptor cells</u>.

2) Effectors can also form part of <u>complex organs</u>.

3) There are <u>two</u> types of effector:

- <u>Muscle cells</u> — which make up <u>muscles</u>.

- <u>Hormone secreting</u> (releasing) <u>cells</u> — which are found in <u>glands</u>.

Don't let the thought of exams play on your nerves...

Don't forget that it's only large animals like mammals and birds that have <u>complex nervous systems</u>.

Nervous Communication

Neurones are nerve cells. They work together to connect up the nervous system. They link receptor cells (e.g. in the ears, eyes and skin) to effector cells (e.g. in muscles and glands).

The Central Nervous System (CNS) Controls the Response

The CNS is a processing centre. This means it receives information from the receptors and then decides what to do about it. For example:

1) A small bird is feeding, when it spots a cat sneaking up on it (a stimulus).

2) Sensory neurones carry the information from the receptors in the bird's eye to the CNS.

3) The CNS decides what to do about it.

4) The CNS sends information to the muscles in the bird's wings (the effectors) along motor neurones.

5) The bird flies away to safety.

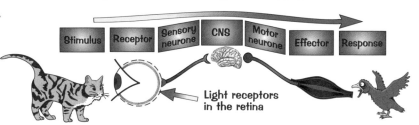

Stimulus → Receptor → Sensory neurone → CNS → Motor neurone → Effector → Response

Light receptors in the retina

Information is Transmitted Around the Body by Neurones

When stimulated, neurones transmit (send) information around the body as electrical impulses.

1) The electrical impulses pass along the axon of the nerve cells.

2) Axons are made from the nerve cell's cytoplasm. It's stretched out into a long fibre and surrounded by a cell membrane.

3) Some are also surrounded by a fatty sheath (covering). This acts as an electrical insulator. It shields the neurone from the cells next to it. This speeds up the electrical impulse.

A typical neurone

Nucleus

Insulating Sheath

Cell body

Axon

4) Electrical impulses travel round the body really quickly. They cause fast, short-lived responses, e.g. pulling your hand away from something hot.

5) Hormones are chemicals that also carry information. Insulin and oestrogen are examples of hormones.

6) They're produced by glands and they travel in the blood. The responses they cause are brought about more slowly. Hormonal responses are longer lasting than the responses caused by nerve impulses.

The Gap Between Two Neurones is Called a Synapse

1) Neurones aren't attached to each other. There's a tiny gap between them called the synapse.

2) Information in one neurone is transmitted across the synapse to the next neurone.

3) Toxins and drugs like ecstasy, beta-blockers and PROZAC® can affect the transmission of impulses across a synapse.

Neurones transmit information from this book to your brain...

Make sure you wrap your head around this stuff on neurones — it'll make the rest of the section a lot easier...

Reflexes

Sometimes waiting for your brain to make a decision is <u>too slow</u> — that's why you're <u>born</u> with <u>reflexes</u>. And if you're a <u>simple animal</u> without a brain, reflexes are pretty much all you can <u>rely on</u>.

Reflexes are Responses That You Don't Think About

1) <u>Reflexes</u> are <u>rapid</u>, <u>automatic</u> responses to certain stimuli.

2) Reflexes are <u>quick</u> because you <u>don't think</u> about them — they're <u>involuntary</u>.

3) The route taken by the information in a reflex (from receptor to effector) is called a <u>reflex arc</u>.

The Reflex Arc Goes Through the Central Nervous System

1) The neurones in reflex arcs go through the <u>spinal cord</u>.

2) When a <u>stimulus</u> (e.g. a painful bee sting) is detected by receptors, an impulse is sent along a <u>sensory neurone</u> to the CNS.

3) In the CNS the sensory neurone passes on the message to another type of neurone — a <u>relay neurone</u>.

4) The relay neurone <u>passes</u> the impulse to a <u>motor neurone</u>.

5) The impulse then travels along the motor neurone to the <u>effector</u>.

6) In this example the effector's a muscle. The <u>muscle</u> <u>contracts</u> and moves your hand away from the bee.

5. Message travels along a motor neurone

4. Message is passed along a relay neurone

CNS

6. When message reaches muscle, it contracts to move arm away from bee

3. Message travels along the sensory neurone

2. Stimulation of the pain receptor

1. Cheeky bee stings finger

Simple Reflexes Improve the Chance of Survival

1) <u>Simple animals</u> have <u>no brain</u> — they rely on <u>simple reflex</u> actions.

2) Simple reflexes cause these animals to <u>respond</u> to some stimuli in a way that <u>helps them survive</u>. For example, reflexes help them <u>find food</u> and <u>shelter from predators</u>.

3) <u>Humans</u> also have <u>simple reflexes</u>. They <u>protect</u> us from damage or increase our chances of <u>survival</u>:

Simple animals are things like jellyfish.

> 1) Very bright <u>light</u> can <u>damage</u> the <u>eye</u> — so there's a reflex to protect it. In very bright light muscles in the eye <u>contract</u>. This makes the <u>pupil smaller</u> and allows <u>less light</u> into the eye.
>
> 2) If a person picks up a <u>hot object</u> there's a reflex that makes them <u>drop</u> it.
>
> 3) <u>Newborn babies</u> have reflexes that are <u>lost</u> as they <u>grow up</u>, for example:
> - they'll <u>automatically suckle</u> from their mothers.
> - they'll <u>grasp</u> when their palms are touched.
> - they'll try to <u>take steps</u> when their feet are put on a flat surface.
>
> 4) Your doctor might have tested your <u>knee jerk reflex</u> by tapping under your knee.

Don't get all twitchy — just learn it...

You <u>don't think about reflexes</u> — they just happen. Revision is not such an automatic process, unfortunately...

Reflexes and Learning

The reflexes that you're born with are pretty handy, but it doesn't stop there — you can <u>learn new ones</u> too.

Reflex Responses can Also be Learned

1) A stimulus causes a certain reflex response.

2) Animals can <u>learn</u> to have the <u>same response</u> to a <u>new stimulus</u> (called a <u>secondary stimulus</u>).

3) This is called <u>conditioning</u>. The new reflex is called a <u>conditioned reflex</u>.

4) You need to know about <u>two examples</u> of <u>conditioning</u>:

Pavlov's Dogs

1) A scientist called Pavlov noticed that dogs <u>salivated</u> (drooled) when they smelt food.

2) This is a <u>simple reflex</u> in response to a <u>primary stimulus</u> (the smell of food).

3) He started ringing a <u>bell</u> just before the dogs were fed.

4) After a while he found that the dogs <u>salivated</u> when the bell was rung — even if they couldn't smell food.

5) The dogs responded to a <u>secondary stimulus</u> (the bell). This is a <u>conditioned reflex</u>.

Predators Avoiding Brightly Coloured Insects

1) Insects with <u>bright colouring</u> are often <u>poisonous</u>.

2) Their bright colours <u>warn predators</u> (such as birds) that they'll probably taste pretty <u>horrible</u> and could cause some <u>harm</u>.

> **EXAMPLE**
> 1) A bird spots a <u>brightly coloured caterpillar</u>.
> 2) When the bird <u>eats</u> the caterpillar it notices that it <u>tastes nasty</u> and makes the bird feel <u>ill</u>.
> 3) The bird <u>links</u> the <u>bad taste</u> and <u>illness</u> with the <u>colour</u>.
> 4) The next time it spots a caterpillar with that colouring, it <u>avoids it</u>.

3) The predators develop a <u>conditioned reflex</u> to the <u>secondary stimulus</u> (the <u>colour</u> of the insects).

Humans are Really Good at Learning

1) The brain is basically <u>billions</u> of <u>neurones</u> all <u>linked up</u>.

2) This means that it can do clever things like:
- change behaviour as a result of experience — i.e. <u>learn stuff</u>.
- control complicated behaviour, e.g. <u>social behaviour</u> (interacting with other people).

3) <u>All animals</u> with <u>brains</u> can <u>learn</u> things.

4) <u>Humans</u> are <u>much better</u> at learning than other animals.

5) This is because we've <u>evolved</u> a much <u>bigger brain</u>.

6) This has given us a <u>survival advantage</u>.

I condition my hair to make it lie down...

If this conditioning stuff pops up in the exam they might not always give you the classic <u>Pavlov</u> example. You just have to <u>apply</u> what you know from learning this wonderful page.

Brain Development and Learning

That great big spongy mass in your head helps you <u>learn useful things</u> like how to walk and talk.
But it also helps with not so useful things like how to play <u>snap</u> and do <u>handstands</u>.

The Environment can Affect Brain Development and Learning

The brain develops at an early age

1) In the brain of a <u>newborn baby</u> most of the <u>neurone connections</u> are <u>not yet formed</u>.

2) <u>Connections form</u> as the child <u>experiences</u> <u>new things</u>.

3) When a neurone is stimulated by a new experience it <u>branches out</u>.
This connects neurones that <u>weren't</u> <u>connected before</u>.

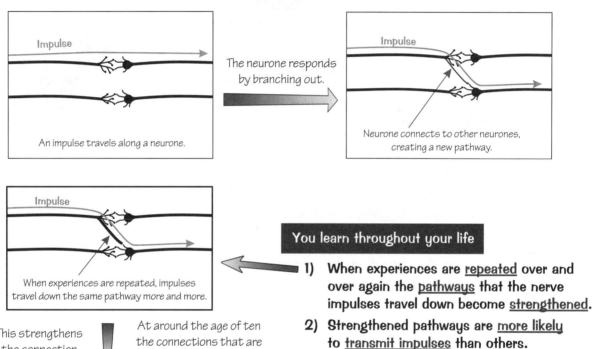

You learn throughout your life

1) When experiences are <u>repeated</u> over and over again the <u>pathways</u> that the nerve impulses travel down become <u>strengthened</u>.

2) Strengthened pathways are <u>more likely</u> to <u>transmit impulses</u> than others.

3) This is why doing things like playing the piano is easier if you've practised a lot.

4) After the age of about ten the pathways that aren't used as often <u>die off</u>.

You Need to Know About the Cerebral Cortex

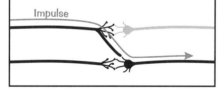

1) The <u>outer part</u> of the brain is called the <u>cerebral cortex</u>.

2) The cerebral cortex is important for things like <u>intelligence</u>, <u>memory</u>, <u>language</u> and <u>consciousness</u> (being aware of things).

The brain — Cerebral cortex

Strengthening pathways — usually done with tarmac...

This stuff is pretty tricky but you need to get your head round it. When you're really young you <u>connect</u> all your neurones. Then the ones you use the most are <u>strengthened</u> and the others <u>die off</u>.

Studying the Brain

Scientists know a bit about the <u>brain</u> but <u>not as much</u> as they'd like to.

Scientists Study the Brain to Find Out Which Bits do What

1) Scientists can study patients with <u>brain damage</u>. E.g. if an area at the back of the brain was damaged and the patient went <u>blind</u> you know that the area has something to do with <u>vision</u>.

2) Scientists can <u>electrically stimulate</u> (activate) different <u>parts of the brain</u>. They can see the effects this has on a patient, e.g. <u>muscles</u> might <u>contract</u>.

3) Scientists can <u>scan</u> the brain, e.g. with an <u>MRI scanner</u>. This shows the <u>structure</u> of the brain. It also shows which <u>parts</u> of the brain are <u>active</u> when a patient is doing different <u>activities</u>, e.g. listening to music.

Memory is the Storage and Retrieval of Information

1) To <u>remember</u> something first you have to <u>store</u> the information (i.e. <u>learn it</u>). Then you have to <u>retrieve</u> it.

2) There are <u>two main types</u> of memory — <u>short-term</u> and <u>long-term</u>:

- <u>Short-term memory</u> lasts for anything from a few <u>seconds</u> to a few <u>hours</u>.
- <u>Long-term memories</u> are memories that were stored <u>days</u>, <u>months</u> or even <u>years</u> ago.

3) Humans are <u>more likely</u> to <u>remember</u> things if:

- They can see a <u>pattern</u> in the information or <u>impose</u> a pattern on it (<u>make up</u> a pattern to <u>remember</u> it). For example, remembering the phone number 123123 is a lot easier than remembering 638294.
- The information is associated (linked) with <u>strong stimuli</u>, like bright lights and colours, strong smells or noises.
- The information is <u>repeated</u>, especially if it's over a <u>long time</u>.

Memory Models Try to Explain How Memory Works

1) There are loads of different <u>models</u> that try to explain <u>how memory works</u>.

2) For example, some scientists think the <u>multi-store model</u> is a good explanation:

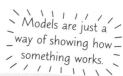
Models are just a way of showing how something works.

Multi-store model	
1) Information that you've <u>paid attention</u> to is <u>temporarily stored</u> in <u>short-term</u> memory.
2) If it's <u>repeated</u> enough it's <u>moved</u> to <u>long-term</u> memory and <u>stored</u> there.
3) Memories that are <u>never moved</u> from the short term memory to the long term memory are <u>forgotten</u>.
4) Information can be <u>retrieved</u> from the long term memory and <u>remembered</u>.

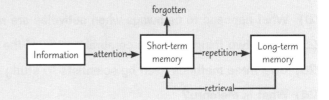

3) So far <u>no model</u> has been able to <u>fully explain</u> how human memory works.

Memory's just like knitting — all you need is a good pattern...

Hopefully this should give you some handy <u>revision tips</u>. <u>Repeating</u> things helps lodge them in your <u>long-term memory</u> and using <u>bright colours</u> means you associate <u>facts</u> with a <u>strong stimulus</u>. Simple.

Revision Summary for Module B6

Hmm... so this whole nervous system and brain business — I'll admit it's not the easiest topic in the world, but it's pretty interesting I reckon. And now you know why the only way to get stuff into your long-term memory for your exam is to repeat it over and over and over and over and over again... and on that note here's some questions to see whether any of the information you've just read has made it into your long-term storage space.

1) What is a stimulus?

2) What are receptors? Give an example of a receptor.

3) Name the two organs that make up the CNS.

4) What do sensory neurones do?

5) Where do motor neurones carry signals to and from?

6) What are effectors? Name two examples of an effector.

7) What is the role of the CNS?

8) Copy and complete the diagram below to show the pathway between a stimulus and a response.

9) How do neurones transmit information?

10) What is an axon?

11) What is the function of the fatty sheath surrounding some axons?

12) What is a synapse?

13) Name two different chemicals that affect the transmission of impulses across synapses.

14) What is a reflex?

15) Describe how information travels along a reflex arc, from a receptor to an effector.

16) Give two ways that simple reflexes increase an animal's chance of survival.

17) Give three examples of simple reflexes in humans.

18) a) What reflex Pavlov did notice in dogs?
    b) How did Pavlov create a conditioned reflex in dogs?

19) Describe another example of a conditioned reflex.

20) How can new experiences increase the number of connections in the brain of a child?

21) What happens to pathways when activities are repeated?

22) Name two things that the cerebral cortex of the brain is important for.

23) Give three methods used by scientists to study the brain.

24) What is memory?

25) According to the multi-store model of memory:
    a) What happens to information in short term memory that's repeated?
    b) Information can be retrieved from long term memory and remembered. True or false?

Atoms

Atoms are the building blocks of <u>everything</u> — and I mean everything. Really...

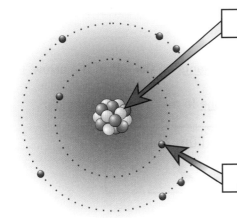

The Nucleus

1) It's in the <u>middle</u> of the atom.

2) It's made up of <u>protons</u> and <u>neutrons</u>.

3) It's <u>tiny</u> compared to the rest of the atom.

The Electrons

1) Move <u>around</u> the nucleus.

2) They're arranged in <u>shells</u> (different levels).

3) They're <u>tiny</u>, but they cover <u>a lot of space</u>.

Know Your Particles...

1) <u>Protons</u> are <u>heavy</u> and <u>positively charged</u>.

2) <u>Neutrons</u> are <u>heavy</u> and <u>neutral</u> (have no charge).

3) <u>Electrons</u> are <u>tiny</u> and <u>negatively charged</u>.

PARTICLE	RELATIVE MASS	CHARGE
Proton	1	+1
Neutron	1	0
Electron	0.0005	-1

Each Element has a Different Number of Protons

1) Atoms of <u>different elements</u> have <u>different numbers of protons</u>.
   For example carbon has 6 protons and nitrogen has 7 protons.

2) <u>All atoms</u> of the <u>same element</u> have the <u>same number of protons</u>.
   So <u>all</u> carbon atoms have 6 protons and <u>all</u> nitrogen atoms have 7 protons.

3) The number of protons an element has is its <u>proton number</u> on the periodic table.

4) The <u>number</u> of <u>protons</u> in an atom is the same as the <u>number</u> of <u>electrons</u>.

Number of protons = number of electrons...

This stuff might seem a bit useless at first, but it should be well and truly stuck in your mind. If you don't know these basic facts, the rest of Chemistry is going to make as much sense as a mouse break dancing to jazz. So <u>learn it now</u>, and watch as the Universe unfolds and reveals its timeless mysteries to you...

Chemical Equations

Every time you see a <u>chemical equation</u> it's showing you a load of information — no really it is...

Chemical Reactions are Shown Using Word Equations...

1) Word equations are an <u>easy</u> way to show what's going on in a reaction. They crop up all over these chemistry sections.

2) To <u>write a word equation</u> you just put the names of the <u>reactants</u> on the <u>left</u> of the arrow and the names of the <u>products</u> on the <u>right</u>.
For example, this is the reaction between <u>sodium</u> and <u>chlorine</u> to make <u>sodium chloride</u>:

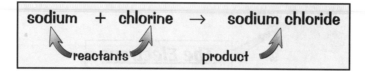

...and Symbol Equations

1) Different <u>chemicals</u> are given different <u>symbols</u>, e.g. sodium is Na and chlorine is Cl.

2) <u>Symbol equations</u> show the atoms at the <u>start</u> (the <u>reactant</u> atoms) and the atoms at the <u>end</u> (the <u>product atoms</u>) and how they're arranged.

3) For example, this is the symbol equation for the reaction between sodium and chlorine:

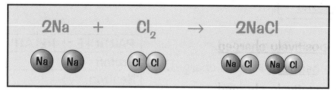

4) Symbol equations show <u>how many atoms</u> of an element there are.
E.g. the little 2 in Cl_2 means there are two Cl atoms.

5) They also show <u>how many molecules</u> or <u>particles</u> of something there are.
E.g. the big 2 in 2NaCl means there are two lots of NaCl.

State Symbols Tell You What Physical State a Chemical is In

State symbols get added to symbol equations to show if the substance is a <u>solid</u>, <u>liquid</u>, <u>gas</u> or is <u>dissolved in water</u> (aqueous).

(s) — Solid   (l) — Liquid   (g) — Gas   (aq) — Dissolved in water

For example:

$$2Na(s) + Cl_2(g) \rightarrow 2NaCl(s)$$

Na is a solid Cl_2 is a gas   NaCl is a solid

This page has left me in a state...

Those <u>numbers</u> in <u>symbol equations</u> mean a lot... A number in <u>front</u> of a formula applies to the <u>entire formula</u>. So, <u>3</u>Na_2SO_4 means three lots of Na_2SO_4. The little numbers in the <u>middle</u> or at the <u>end</u> of a formula <u>only</u> apply to the atom <u>immediately before</u>. So the 4 in Na_2SO_4 just means 4 O's, not 4 S's.

Line Spectrums

Colour isn't just to do with art — you've got to learn about it in Chemistry too.

Some Elements Give Off Colours When Heated

1) When elements like <u>lithium</u>, <u>sodium</u> and <u>potassium</u> are heated
   they produce a <u>coloured flame</u>.

2) These colours are often <u>distinctive</u> (easy to spot) so you can
   use them to work out what the element is.

All the different colours seen in fireworks are due to the colours
produced by different elements — it's a great bit of chemistry.

Each Element Gives a Different Line Spectrum

1) A clever way to identify an element is to look at the exact colour it makes in a flame using a <u>line spectrum</u>.

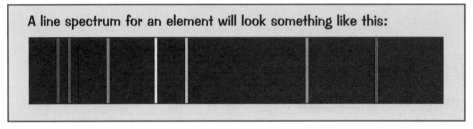

A line spectrum for an element will look something like this:

2) Different <u>elements</u> give off different <u>colours</u>.

3) This means they'll produce <u>different line spectrums</u>.

4) Each element will make a <u>characteristic line spectrum</u> — the lines are <u>always</u> in the
   same place for that element.

5) So you can <u>identify</u> an element (find out what it is) by looking at its line spectrum.

Line Spectrums Have Been Used to Identify New Elements

1) Making and looking at line spectrums is called <u>spectroscopy</u>.

2) Spectroscopy has let scientists <u>discover new elements</u>.

3) Some of these elements wouldn't have been discovered without <u>new practical</u>
   <u>techniques</u> like spectroscopy.

When scientists discover something
it means they've found something
that's never been found before.

Spectroscopy — it's a flaming useful technique...

This is quite a clever way of <u>identifying</u> elements. I know it's a bit tricky, but make sure you learn that
<u>different elements</u> produce <u>different colours</u> and <u>line spectrums</u> (the lines are in different places).
More importantly, we've been able to <u>find new elements</u> (that might still be unknown) using spectroscopy.

History of the Periodic Table

The periodic table is a mighty useful way of sorting the elements. You need to know about the scientists Döboroinor, Newlands and Mendeleev, and how their ideas were used to create the periodic table.

1) Döbereiner Tried to Sort Elements into Threes

1) Döbereiner put the elements into groups of three, which he called triads. E.g. Cl, Br and I were one triad, and Li, Na and K were another.
2) The elements in a triad all had similar chemical properties.
3) The middle element of each triad had a relative atomic mass that was exactly halfway between the other two.

Element	Relative atomic mass	
Lithium	7	difference = 16
Sodium	23	difference = 16
Potassium	39	

2) Newlands' Law of Octaves Was the First Good Effort

H	Li	Be	B	C	N	O
F	Na	Mg	Al	Si	P	S
Cl	K	Ca	Cr	Ti	Mn	Fe

1) Newlands put the elements in order of relative atomic mass.
2) He spotted that every eighth element had similar properties.
3) So he split the elements into rows so that elements with similar properties were lined up.

4) But on the third row, it started to go a bit wrong with metals like iron (Fe) messing up the pattern.

3) Mendeleev Predicted New Elements to Fill Gaps in His Table

1) Mendeleev put the elements in order of atomic mass (like Newlands did).
2) But he left some gaps in the table.
3) This meant that elements with similar properties were in the same vertical groups.
4) He predicted that elements that hadn't been discovered yet would fit into the gaps.
5) When they were found and they fitted the pattern it helped convince other scientists that the elements could be put in an order.

Mendeleev's Table of the Elements — vertical group

H																	
Li	Be											B	C	N	O	F	
Na	Mg											Al	Si	P	S	Cl	
K	Ca	*	Ti	V	Cr	Mn	Fe	Co	Ni	Cu	Zn	*	*	As	Se	Br	
Rb	Sr	Y	Zr	Nb	Mo	*	Ru	Rh	Pd	Ag	Cd	In	Sn	Sb	Te	I	
Cs	Ba	*	*	Ta	W	*	Os	Ir	Pt	Au	Hg	Tl	Pb	Bi			

6) For example, he predicted that germanium would have an atomic mass of 72. It turned out that its atomic mass was 73. So he was pretty close.

At First Scientists Didn't Think The Elements Could be Put in Order

1) Scientists started off thinking that there wasn't a link between the relative atomic mass of an element and its chemical properties (like melting point and reactivity).
2) So many of the ideas (theories) put forward were ignored by other scientists.
3) But when Mendeleev used his table to correctly predict the properties of undiscovered elements everybody started to think it was a good idea.

Julie Andrews' octaves — do-re-mi-fa-so-la-ti-do...

So there it is. It took a long time for people to catch on to the idea of sorting the elements. And even longer before they came up with the periodic table as we know it today. To see what that's like, turn to the next page.

The Modern Periodic Table

After all that history I present the periodic table — a chemist's best friend... seriously...

The Periodic Table Puts Elements with Similar Properties Together

1) In the periodic table the elements are put in <u>order</u> of <u>proton number</u>.

2) This creates <u>patterns</u> in the elements that <u>repeat</u> across the table, e.g. how they react.

3) <u>Metals</u> are found on the <u>left</u> and <u>non-metals</u> on the <u>right</u>.

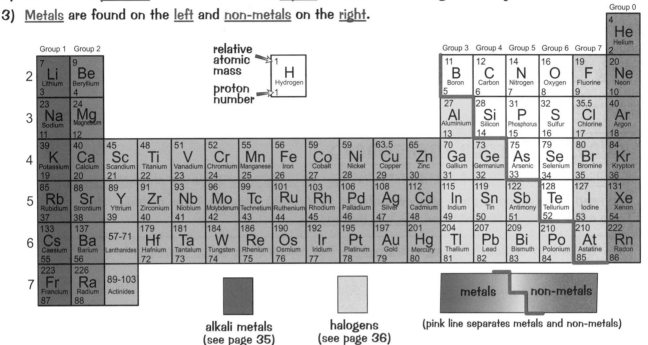

alkali metals
(see page 35)

halogens
(see page 36)

(pink line separates metals and non-metals)

4) The <u>rows across</u> are called <u>periods</u>. So Li, Be, B, C, N, O, F and Ne are all in the same period.

5) The <u>vertical columns</u> are called <u>groups</u> — they have elements with <u>similar properties</u> in them.
For example, the <u>Group 1</u> elements are all <u>metals</u> and they all <u>react in a similar way</u> (see page 35).

6) The <u>group number</u> tells you how many <u>electrons</u> there are in the <u>outer shell</u>.
For example, <u>Group 1</u> elements all have <u>one</u> electron in their outer shell and <u>Group 7</u> all have <u>seven</u>
electrons in their outer shell. Easy.

7) The only group number that doesn't tell you this is <u>Group 0</u>
— the Group 0 elements all have <u>8 electrons</u> in their outer shell.

8) If you know the <u>properties</u> of <u>one element</u>, you can <u>predict</u> properties of <u>other elements</u> in that group.
So, if you know sodium forms <u>ionic bonds</u> then you can predict that potassium will too.

You Can Get Loads of Information from the Periodic Table

By looking at the table, you can find out straight away:

1) The <u>name</u> and <u>symbol</u> of each element.

2) The <u>proton number</u> of each element.

3) The <u>relative atomic mass</u> of each element.

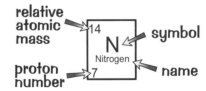

I'm in a chemistry band — I play the symbols...

You <u>don't</u> need to know the properties of each group of the periodic table. But if you're told, for example, that
fluorine (Group 7) forms <u>two-atom molecules</u>, it's a fair guess that chlorine, bromine, iodine and astatine <u>do too</u>.

Electron Shells

Electron shells... the things electrons zoom about in.

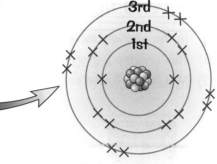

Electron Shell Rules:

1) Electrons are in <u>shells</u> around the nucleus.
2) These shells are sometimes called <u>energy levels</u>.
3) The <u>inner</u> shells are <u>always filled first</u>.
4) Only <u>a certain number</u> of electrons are allowed in each shell:

<u>1st shell</u>: 2   <u>2nd Shell</u>: 8   <u>3rd Shell</u>: 8

(Each cross is an electron.)

Working Out Electron Arrangements

1) The <u>electron arrangement</u> of an atom tells you <u>how many electrons</u> there are and <u>which shells</u> they're in.

2) You need to know the electron arrangements for the <u>first 20</u> elements in the periodic table.
For a quick example, take nitrogen. <u>Follow these steps</u>...

1) The proton number for nitrogen is <u>seven</u> — this means it has <u>seven electrons</u>.
2) The <u>first</u> shell can only take <u>2</u> electrons — so put 2 in the first shell.
3) This leaves <u>5</u> for the <u>second</u> shell.
4) So the electron arrangement for nitrogen must be <u>2, 5</u> — easy peasy.

Nitrogen

3) Now <u>you</u> try it for argon (see the box below for the answer).

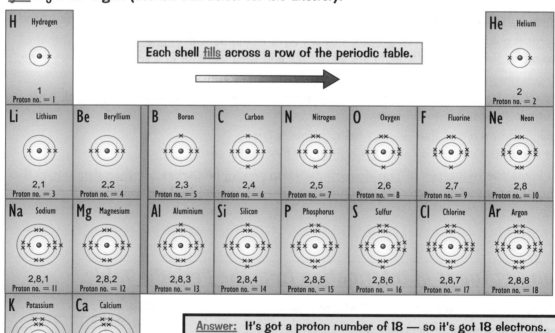

Each shell <u>fills</u> across a row of the periodic table.

H Hydrogen							He Helium
1 Proton no. = 1							2 Proton no. = 2
Li Lithium	Be Beryllium	B Boron	C Carbon	N Nitrogen	O Oxygen	F Fluorine	Ne Neon
2,1 Proton no. = 3	2,2 Proton no. = 4	2,3 Proton no. = 5	2,4 Proton no. = 6	2,5 Proton no. = 7	2,6 Proton no. = 8	2,7 Proton no. = 9	2,8 Proton no. = 10
Na Sodium	Mg Magnesium	Al Aluminium	Si Silicon	P Phosphorus	S Sulfur	Cl Chlorine	Ar Argon
2,8,1 Proton no. = 11	2,8,2 Proton no. = 12	2,8,3 Proton no. = 13	2,8,4 Proton no. = 14	2,8,5 Proton no. = 15	2,8,6 Proton no. = 16	2,8,7 Proton no. = 17	2,8,8 Proton no. = 18
K Potassium	Ca Calcium						
2,8,8,1 Proton no. = 19	2,8,8,2 Proton no. = 20						

<u>Answer:</u> It's got a proton number of 18 — so it's got 18 electrons.
- The first shell must have <u>2</u> electrons.
- The second shell must have <u>8</u>.
- The third shell must have <u>8</u> as well.

So its electron arrangement is <u>2, 8, 8</u>.   Argon

One little duck and two fat ladies — 2, 8, 8...

You need to know enough about electron shells to draw out that <u>whole diagram</u> at the bottom of the page without looking at it. Obviously, you don't have to learn each element separately — just <u>learn the pattern</u>.

Ionic Bonding

This stuff's a bit tricky — but don't worry. Just take it nice and slow and you'll get it...

Ions Are Made when Atoms Gain or Lose Electrons

1) Atoms can lose or gain electrons.
2) When this happens the atom forms a charged particle called an ion.
3) Negative ions are shown using a little minus sign ($^-$) and positive ions are shown using a little plus sign ($^+$).
4) Ions can be made from single atoms, e.g. the Cl^- ion.
5) They can also be made from groups of atoms, e.g. the NO_3^- ion.
6) When atoms lose or gain electrons, all they're trying to do is get a full outer shell.

Group 1 Elements Lose Electrons

1) All the atoms in Group 1 of the periodic table have just one electron in their outer shell.
2) They want to get rid of it by giving it to something else.
3) When Group 1 elements lose an electron they form positive ions.

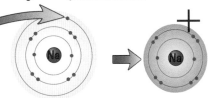

The sodium atom gives up its outer electron and becomes an Na^+ ion.

Group 7 Elements Gain Electrons

1) On the other side of the periodic table, the elements in Group 7 have outer shells that are nearly full.
2) They want to gain one electron to get a full outer shell.
3) When Group 7 elements gain an electron they form negative ions.

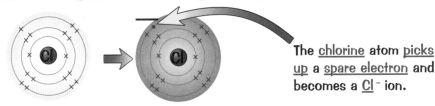

The chlorine atom picks up a spare electron and becomes a Cl^- ion.

Ionic Bonding — Group 1 and Group 7 Elements

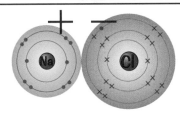

1) Compounds formed between Group 1 and Group 7 elements are ionic.
2) The reaction of sodium and chlorine is a classic case.
3) Chlorine gains the electron that sodium gives away.
4) The positive sodium ion and the negative chloride ion form an ionic bond.

Forming ions — seems like the trendy thing to do...

Remember, the positive and negative charges we talk about (e.g. Na^+ for sodium) just tell you what type of ion the atom WILL FORM in a chemical reaction. In sodium metal there are only neutral sodium atoms, Na. The Na^+ ions will only appear if the sodium metal reacts with something like water or chlorine.

Ionic Compounds

Those <u>ionic compounds</u> that were made on the previous page do some weird stuff. Just look at this...

Ionic Compounds **Form a Lattice**

1) Solid ionic compounds like <u>sodium chloride</u> form crystals.

2) This is because the positive and negative ions are arranged in a <u>regular lattice</u>.

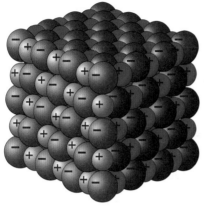

In a regular lattice the ions are stacked neatly next to each other and not all over the place.

"Regular lettuce."

Ionic Compounds **Split Up** When **Dissolved** or **Molten**

1) All the ions in the regular lattice are held in a <u>fixed</u> place.

2) The bonds that hold the ions in place are <u>ionic bonds</u>.

3) When an ionic compound is <u>dissolved</u> or <u>melted</u> the ions are <u>free to move</u>.

4) Because they can move around they can <u>conduct electricity</u>.

Dissolved

Melted

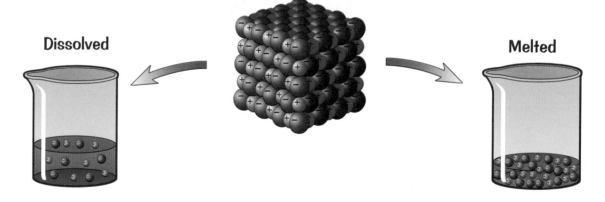

5) The fact that molten <u>compounds</u> of <u>metals</u> and <u>non-metals</u> can conduct electricity is <u>evidence</u> that they're made up of <u>ions</u>.

Any old ion, any old ion — any, any, any old ion...

I said those ionic compounds did some weird stuff. The giant <u>lattices</u> they form are <u>regular</u> — that just means they're cube shaped and not some strange blob shape. Also remember that ionic compounds can only <u>conduct</u> electricity when they are <u>dissolved</u> or <u>molten</u> because that's when the ions are freeeeeeeeeeeeeee...

Group 1 — The Alkali Metals

Alkali metals are all members of the same group — Group 1.

Group 1 Metals are Known as the 'Alkali Metals'

1) Group 1 metals include lithium (Li), sodium (Na) and potassium (K)... know these names really well.

2) When the alkali metals react they all form similar compounds.

3) The alkali metals are shiny when they're cut.

4) But they quickly tarnish (lose their shininess) by reacting with oxygen and moisture in the air.

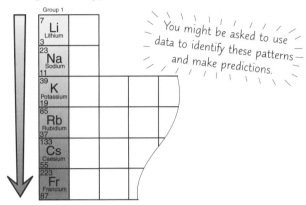

As you go DOWN Group 1, the alkali metals:

1) become MORE REACTIVE (see below)

2) have a HIGHER DENSITY

3) have a LOWER MELTING POINT

4) have a LOWER BOILING POINT

These patterns are sometimes called 'trends'.

You might be asked to use data to identify these patterns and make predictions.

Reaction with Cold Water Produces Hydrogen Gas

Vigorously means fast and with a lot of oomph.

1) When lithium, sodium or potassium are put in water (H_2O) they react vigorously.

2) They move around the surface, fizzing loads and producing hydrogen gas (H_2).

3) The reaction makes an alkaline solution — this is why Group 1 is known as the alkali metals.

4) A hydroxide of the metal forms e.g. lithium hydroxide (LiOH), sodium hydroxide (NaOH) or potassium hydroxide (KOH).

5) As you go down Group 1 the reaction becomes more violent. This is because the alkali metals become more reactive.

6) So lithium is the least reactive and will fizz in water, but caesium is much more reactive and will explode.

Reaction with Chlorine Produces Salts

1) Alkali metals react vigorously with chlorine.

2) The reaction produces colourless salt crystals, e.g. lithium chloride (LiCl), sodium chloride (NaCl) and potassium chloride (KCl).

3) Again the reaction gets more vigorous as you go down the group.

Fizzzzzzzzzzzzzzzzzzzzzzzzzzzzzzzzzzzzzzzzzzzzzzzzzz...

Alkali metals are ace. They're so reactive you have to store them in oil — because otherwise they'd react with the water in the air. AND they fizz in water and explode and everything. Cool.

Group 7 — Halogens

The 'trend thing' happens in Group 7 as well — no surprise there.

Group 7 Elements are Known as the Halogens

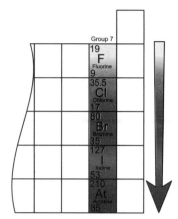

1) Group 7 elements include <u>chlorine</u> (Cl), <u>bromine</u> (Br) and <u>iodine</u> (I).

2) The halogens form <u>diatomic molecules</u> which are <u>pairs of atoms</u>.

          I_2

3) As you go <u>DOWN</u> Group 7, the halogens:

- become <u>LESS REACTIVE</u> (see below)

- have a <u>HIGHER MELTING POINT</u>

- have a <u>HIGHER BOILING POINT</u>

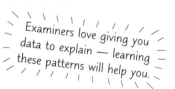

Examiners love giving you data to explain — learning these patterns will help you.

The Halogens are All Coloured Non-metals

1) <u>Fluorine</u> is a <u>yellow gas</u> at room temperature.

2) <u>Chlorine</u> is a <u>green gas</u> at room temperature.

3) <u>Bromine</u> is an <u>orange liquid</u> at room temperature and forms an <u>orange gas</u>.

4) <u>Iodine</u> is a <u>dark grey solid</u> at room temperature or a <u>purple gas</u>.

Halogens become Less Reactive Down the Group

<u>Chlorine</u> is more reactive than <u>bromine</u>, which is more reactive than <u>iodine</u>. This <u>trend</u> in reactivity can be shown by looking at different <u>reactions</u>.

REACTIONS WITH ALKALI METALS AND IRON

1) The halogens will react with <u>alkali metals</u> (e.g. Li, Na, K) and <u>iron</u> (Fe).

2) The reactions become <u>less vigorous</u> as you go <u>down the group</u>.

DISPLACEMENT REACTIONS

1) A <u>more</u> reactive element '<u>pushes out</u>' (displaces) a <u>less</u> reactive element from a compound.

2) <u>Chlorine</u> is <u>most reactive</u> so pushes out bromine and iodine from their compounds. E.g. chlorine will <u>replace</u> iodine in potassium iodide. Potassium chloride will be formed. Iodine will be left on its own.

3) <u>Bromine</u> is <u>more reactive</u> than <u>iodine</u> so will push it out of compounds.

They're great, the halogens — you have to hand it to them...

The halogens are another group from the periodic table, and just like the alkali metals (see page 35) you've got to learn their trends and the reactions on this page. <u>Learn</u> them, <u>cover</u> up the page, <u>scribble</u>, <u>check</u>.

Laboratory Safety

<u>Safety</u> is an important thing — it seems everything is out to get you in a lab...

You Need to Learn the Common Hazard Symbols...

If a chemical is <u>bad for you</u> or <u>dangerous</u> in some way it'll have a <u>hazard symbol</u> on it telling you <u>how</u> it could be harmful. These hazard symbols might just save your skin...

Oxidising
<u>Provides oxygen</u> which lets materials <u>burn more strongly</u> — keep away from flames.

Explosive
Can <u>explode</u> — BANG.

Highly Flammable
<u>Catches fire</u> easily — keep away from flames.

Corrosive
<u>Attacks and destroys living tissues</u>, e.g. your eyes and skin.

Toxic
<u>Can cause death</u> if it's swallowed, breathed in, or absorbed through the skin.

...And Know How to Work Safely with Dangerous Chemicals

You need to take <u>safety precautions</u> when you're working with elements like the alkali metals and the halogens. The usual '<u>wear safety specs</u>' goes without saying...

Alkali Metals

The Group 1 elements react with <u>water</u>.

1) They're stored in <u>oil</u> to stop them reacting with water in the air.

2) The <u>sweat</u> on your skin is enough to cause a reaction — so don't touch them with bare hands.

3) All the equipment you use needs to be completely <u>dry</u>.

4) The <u>alkaline</u> solutions they form are <u>corrosive</u> so make sure they don't touch the <u>eyes</u> or the <u>skin</u>.

Halogens

1) <u>Chlorine</u> and <u>iodine</u> are both very <u>toxic</u>.

2) Liquid <u>bromine</u> is <u>corrosive</u> — so you mustn't get it on your skin.

3) Halogens give off <u>poisonous gases</u> that affect your lungs and eyes.
   They must be used inside a <u>fume cupboard</u> so that you don't breathe in the fumes.

No, it means 'oxidising' — not a guy with a wacky hairstyle...

The stuff on this page is all pretty important, not just for passing your exam but also for when you're doing <u>experiments</u> with chemicals in the lab. Make sure you know what the <u>hazard symbols</u> on the containers of chemicals mean — they're not just there to look pretty...

Revision Summary for Module C4

Okay, if you were just about to turn the page without doing these revision summary questions, then stop. What kind of an attitude is that... Is that really the way you want to live your life... running, playing and having fun... Of course not. That's right. Do the questions. It's for the best all round.

1)   What is in the nucleus of an atom?

2)   What is the relative mass of a neutron? What is the charge of a neutron?

3)* How many H atoms are there on the left hand side of this equation?
     $CH_4 + 2O_2 \rightarrow CO_2 + 2H_2O$

4)   Write out the four state symbols and what they mean.

5)   Describe how heating a metal can help to identify it.

6)   What size groups did Döbereiner organise the elements into? What were these groups called?

7)   Why did Mendeleev leave gaps in his Table of Elements?

8)   What can you say about the properties of elements in the same group?

9)   What are the rows in the periodic table known as?

10)* Oxygen can be written as $^{16}_{8}O$. What is the proton number of oxygen?

11) How many electrons can the first shell of any atom hold?

12) Draw the electron arrangement of carbon.

13) Do Group 1 atoms form positive ions or negative ions?

14) Do Group 7 atoms want to gain or lose an electron?

15) What happens to an ionic compound when it is dissolved or melted?

16) Which group are the alkali metals?

17) As you go down the group of alkali metals, do they become more or less reactive?

18) What gas is made when alkali metals react with water?

19) Molecules of Group 7 elements are diatomic. What is a diatomic molecule?

20) Do the Group 7 elements become more or less reactive as you go down the group?

21) Describe what chlorine is like at room temperature.

22) Describe a reaction that can be used to show which halogen is the most reactive.

23) What does this hazard symbol mean?

24) Give two safety precautions you should take when working with alkali metals.

Chemicals in the Air

Welcome to the next section of wonderful Chemistry. Let's kick off with the what's in the <u>air</u> which is also called the <u>atmosphere</u>.

Dry Air is a Mixture of Gases

1) The Earth's atmosphere contains lots of <u>gases</u>.

2) Some of these gases are <u>elements</u> — they're made up of only <u>one type of atom</u>, e.g. oxygen (O_2), nitrogen (N_2) and argon (Ar).

3) Other gases are <u>compounds</u> — they contain <u>more than one type of atom</u> e.g. carbon dioxide (CO_2).

4) Most of the gases in the atmosphere are <u>molecular substances</u> (see below).

Gas	Symbol	Percentage in Air
oxygen	O_2	21%
nitrogen	N_2	78%
argon	Ar	1%
carbon dioxide	CO_2	0.04%

Molecular Substances Have Low Melting and Boiling Points

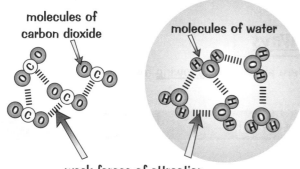

molecules of carbon dioxide

molecules of water

weak forces of attraction

1) <u>Molecular substances</u> are usually <u>small molecules</u>, like CO_2 and H_2O.

2) The <u>forces</u> that attract one molecule to another are <u>very weak</u>.

3) So, you only need a <u>little bit of energy</u> to <u>break</u> the weak forces between the molecules.

4) This means molecular substances have <u>low melting and boiling points</u>.

5) And that means that they're usually <u>gases or liquids</u> at room temperature.

6) Pure molecular substances <u>don't conduct electricity</u> because their molecules aren't <u>charged</u>.

7) Most <u>non-metal elements</u> and most <u>compounds</u> formed from them are <u>molecular</u>.

You Have to be Able to Understand Data

Here's an example exam question — you're given some data and need to <u>interpret it</u> (work out what it means).

Example: Which of the substances in the table is a <u>liquid</u> at room temperature (25 °C)?

	melting point	boiling point
oxygen	-219 °C	-183 °C
nitrogen	-210 °C	-196 °C
bromine	-7 °C	59 °C
argon	-189 °C	-186 °C

• Only <u>bromine</u> fits the description.

• It <u>melts</u> (turns to a liquid) at <u>–7 °C</u> and <u>boils</u> (turns to a gas) at <u>59 °C</u>.

• So, it'll be a <u>liquid</u> at room temperature.

• <u>Oxygen</u>, <u>nitrogen</u> and <u>argon</u> will be <u>gases</u> at room temperature.

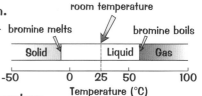

room temperature

bromine melts   bromine boils

| Solid | Liquid | Gas |

-50   0   25   50   100

Temperature (°C)

Stop gassing about it — and get learning...

So, the key things here are those <u>weak forces</u> that join the separate molecules together. They give simple molecular compounds <u>low melting and boiling</u> points, making them likely to be <u>liquids</u> and <u>gases</u> at room temperature.

Covalent Bonding

Some elements form ionic bonds (see page 33), but others form strong <u>covalent bonds</u>.

Bonding in Molecular Substances is Covalent

1) The <u>atoms</u> in small molecular substances are <u>joined</u> together by <u>covalent bonds</u>.
2) These are <u>much much stronger</u> than the weak forces between the molecules (see previous page).

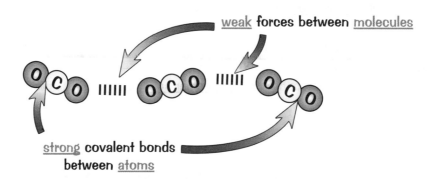

weak forces between <u>molecules</u>

<u>strong</u> covalent bonds
between <u>atoms</u>

Molecules Can Be Shown In Different Ways

Molecular formulas, displayed formulas and 3-D models are all ways of <u>showing</u> molecules.
Here are some examples of each.

	Molecular Formula	2-D 'displayed formula'	3-D model
Oxygen	O_2	$O=O$	
Methane	CH_4	$\begin{array}{c} H \\ \mid \\ H-C-H \\ \mid \\ H \end{array}$	

The <u>molecular formula</u>
shows which <u>atoms</u>
are <u>present</u>.

The 2-D '<u>displayed formula</u>'
shows the <u>atoms</u> and <u>covalent</u>
<u>bonds</u> — so you can tell how
the atoms are joined together.

The 3-D model shows the
<u>atoms</u>, the <u>covalent bonds</u> and
their <u>arrangement</u> in space.

E.g. there are four H
atoms in methane.

E.g. the two atoms in
an oxygen molecule are
joined by a double bond.

E.g. a methane molecule
doesn't lie flat, but has a sort
of triangular pyramid shape.

Where have my 3-D glasses gone...

Make sure you understand that <u>bonding</u> between atoms in molecules is <u>covalent</u>, and the <u>three</u> ways to
show a molecule. You might be shown a molecule one way and then be asked to show it in another.
So make sure you can draw the molecular formula of H–O–H, or a 3-D model of Cl–Cl.

Module C5 — Chemicals of the Natural Environment

Chemicals in the Hydrosphere

The oceans are packed with fish, whales, jellyfish and also plenty of chemicals. Read and learn...

The Earth's Hydrosphere is the Oceans

1) The Earth's hydrosphere is all the water in the oceans, seas, lakes, rivers, puddles and so on...
2) It includes any compounds that are dissolved in the water, like salts.
3) Examples of salts are sodium chloride, magnesium chloride and potassium bromide.
4) Salts are ionic compounds.

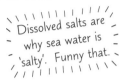
Dissolved salts are why sea water is 'salty'. Funny that.

Solid Ionic Compounds Form Crystals

1) Ionic compounds are made of charged particles called ions.
2) Ions with opposite charges are strongly attracted to one another.
3) This attraction is called an ionic bond — it holds the ions together.
4) All the ions form a massive giant lattice with a regular structure.

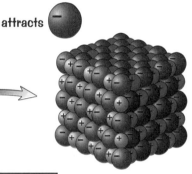
attracts

Ionic Compounds Have High Melting and Boiling Points

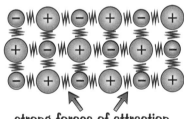
strong forces of attraction

1) Ionic bonds are very strong.
2) So it takes a lot of energy to break these bonds and melt the compound, and even more energy to boil it.
3) This means ionic compounds have high melting and boiling points, which makes them solids at room temperature.

They Conduct Electricity When Dissolved or Molten

1) When an ionic compound dissolves, the ions separate and are all free to move in the solution.
2) This means that they can carry an electric current.
3) When an ionic compound melts, the ions are also free to move. So melted ionic compounds can also carry an electric current.
4) When an ionic compound is a solid, the ions aren't free to move. So an electrical current can't pass through the substance.

Solid

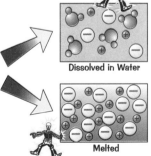
Dissolved in Water

Melted

Giant ionic lattices — all over your chips...

Because they conduct electricity when they're dissolved in water, ionic compounds are used to make some types of battery. In the olden days, most batteries had actual liquid in, so they tended to leak all over the place. Now they've come up with a sort of paste that doesn't leak but still conducts. Clever.

Identifying Positive Ions

Say you've got a compound, but you <u>don't know</u> what it is. Well, you might want to <u>identify</u> it. And that's what the next couple of pages are all about. Tests for <u>positive ions</u> first...

Flame Tests — Spot the Colour

1) One way to <u>identify metal ions</u> is with <u>flame tests</u> (also see page 29).

2) <u>Different ions</u> give <u>different colours</u> when they burn.
For example:

<u>Sodium</u>, Na^+, gives an orange/yellow flame.

<u>Potassium</u>, K^+, gives a lilac flame.

<u>Calcium</u>, Ca^{2+}, gives a brick-red flame.

<u>Copper</u>, Cu^{2+}, gives a blue-green flame.

Add Sodium Hydroxide and Look for a Coloured Precipitate

1) Another way to identify metal ions, if they're <u>dissolved</u>, is to add an alkali like <u>sodium hydroxide</u>.

2) They can react to form an insoluble <u>solid</u> compound called a <u>precipitate</u>.

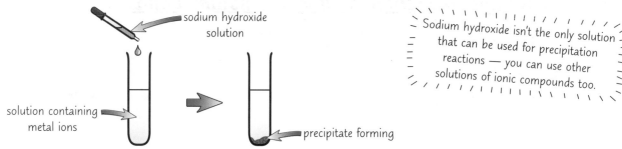

sodium hydroxide solution

solution containing metal ions

precipitate forming

Sodium hydroxide isn't the only solution that can be used for precipitation reactions — you can use other solutions of ionic compounds too.

3) Different metal ions give different <u>coloured hydroxide precipitates</u> when an alkali is added.

4) You might get asked to <u>identify</u> a metal ion by using these results.

"Metal"	Colour of precipitate
Calcium, Ca^{2+}	White
Copper(II), Cu^{2+}	Blue
Iron(II), Fe^{2+}	Sludgy green
Iron(III), Fe^{3+}	Reddish brown
Zinc, Zn^{2+}	White at first. But if even more sodium hydroxide is added it dissolves again to form a colourless solution.

You'll be given a table a bit like this in the exam.

Example: Which metal ions are in the following solutions?

a) Solution A — reddish brown precipitate formed when sodium hydroxide added.

b) Solution B — white precipitate formed when sodium hydroxide added. Nothing changed when more sodium hydroxide was added.

Answer:
a) Solution A — iron(III) ions.
b) Solution B — calcium ions.

It isn't any old ion — get a positive identification...

You've got to keep positive about learning all these tests. The <u>flame tests</u> have already popped up in a previous section. In the exam you'll get a <u>table</u> with the results of testing with <u>sodium hydroxide</u>. But you still need to be able to do a bit of detective work and use those results to work out which positive ions are present.

Identifying Negative Ions

It's not just positive ions you can identify. Yep, you can also identify <u>negative ions</u>. They're often tested for by adding a <u>reagent</u> (a chemical that will react) and looking for an <u>insoluble solid</u> — so the fun goes on...

Hydrochloric Acid Can Help Identify Carbonates

With dilute <u>hydrochloric acid</u>, <u>carbonates</u> (CO_3^{2-}) will fizz because they give off <u>carbon dioxide</u>.

You can test for carbon dioxide using <u>limewater</u>.

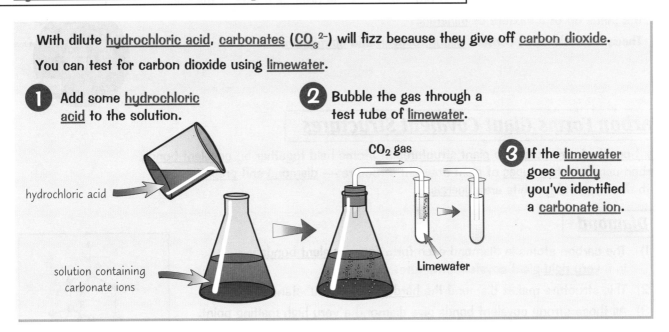

1 Add some <u>hydrochloric acid</u> to the solution.

2 Bubble the gas through a test tube of <u>limewater</u>.

3 If the <u>limewater</u> goes <u>cloudy</u> you've identified a <u>carbonate ion</u>.

hydrochloric acid

solution containing carbonate ions

CO₂ gas

Limewater

Tests for Sulfates (SO_4^{2-}) and Halides (Cl⁻, Br⁻, I⁻) Make Precipitates

Another way to identify negative ions is to add some <u>barium chloride solution</u> or <u>silver nitrate solution</u> and look for a <u>precipitate</u>.

The table below shows <u>which ions</u> each solution <u>tests for</u>, and the <u>colour</u> of the precipitate that forms.

You might get asked to work out the <u>negative ion</u> in a solution using a table like this.

What you add	Ion present in your solution	Colour of precipitate
barium chloride solution	sulfate ion (SO_4^{2-})	white precipitate
silver nitrate solution	chloride ion (Cl⁻)	white precipitate
	bromide ion (Br⁻)	cream precipitate
	iodide ion (I⁻)	yellow precipitate

Example:

Which metal ions are in the following solutions?

a) Solution A — white precipitate formed when barium chloride solution added.

b) Solution B — cream precipitate formed when silver nitrate added.

Answer: a) Solution A — sulfate ions.
b) Solution B — bromide ions.

Don't panic. If you get one of these questions in the exam they'll give you a table a bit like this one.

These tests just detect negative ions — not happy cheery ones...

Make sure you understand the tests on this page — but don't stare at it till your eyes swim and you don't want to see the word "precipitate" ever again. It's been handily divided into <u>two sections</u>, so learn it that way.

Chemicals in the Lithosphere

So, we've done the skies and the seas. Now it's on to the hard stuff (the land, not the work...).

The Earth's Lithosphere is Made Up of a Mixture of Minerals

1) The lithosphere is the Earth's rigid outer layer — the crust and part of the mantle below it.
2) It's made up of a mixture of minerals.
3) These minerals often contain silicon, oxygen and aluminium.

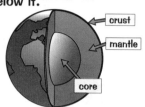

Carbon Forms Giant Covalent Structures

Giant covalent structures are giant structures of atoms held together by covalent bonds.
Carbon can form two types of giant covalent structure — diamond and graphite.
Both diamond and graphite are minerals.

Diamond

1) The carbon atoms in diamond each form four covalent bonds in a very rigid giant covalent structure.
2) This structure makes diamond the hardest natural substance.
3) All those strong covalent bonds give diamond a very high melting point.
4) It doesn't conduct electricity because it has no free electrons.
5) It's insoluble in water.

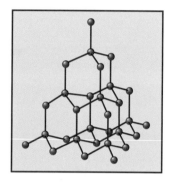

Graphite

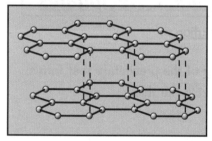

1) Graphite has a different giant covalent structure.
2) Each carbon atom only forms three covalent bonds.
3) This makes sheets of carbon atoms with free electrons between them.
4) The sheets can slide over each other. This makes graphite slippery and soft. It leaves marks on paper so can be used in pencils.
5) Graphite also has a high melting point — the covalent bonds need loads of energy to break.
6) Graphite is different to diamond because it has free electrons so it can conduct electricity.

Silicon Dioxide is Also a Giant Covalent Structure

1) Most of the silicon and oxygen in the Earth's crust forms silicon dioxide.
2) Silicon dioxide is one giant structure of silicon and oxygen.
3) Silicon dioxide has a similar structure to diamond so has similar properties.
   E.g. it has a high melting point and doesn't conduct electricity.

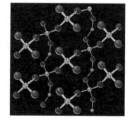

Don't forget your minerals — and your vitamins too...

So, all that stuff beneath your feet is packed full of minerals and loads of it contains elements like silicon, oxygen and aluminium. You might get asked about which type of mineral has the most silicon or the most aluminium. But don't panic, you'll be given you a table with all the information in so you can work it out. Phew.

Metals from Minerals

You don't find many big lumps of <u>metal</u> in the ground — the metal atoms tend to be joined to other atoms in <u>compounds</u>. It can be tricky to <u>separate</u> the metal from the other atoms in the compound.

Ores Contain Enough Metal to Make Extraction Worthwhile

1) <u>Rocks</u> are made of <u>minerals</u>. Minerals are just <u>solid elements and compounds</u>.

2) <u>Metal ores</u> are <u>rocks</u> that contain <u>minerals</u> that metals can be <u>extracted</u> from.

3) The amount of <u>valuable</u> (useful) <u>mineral</u> in the rock can be a <u>very small percentage</u>.

4) For example <u>lots</u> of <u>copper ore</u> needs to be mined to get a <u>small amount</u> of <u>copper</u>.

Some Metals can be Extracted by Heating with Carbon

1) Lots of <u>ores</u> are <u>oxides</u>, e.g. iron is extracted from iron oxide.

2) A common way of <u>extracting</u> (removing) <u>a metal</u> from its oxide ore is by heating it with some <u>carbon</u>.

3) The ore is <u>REDUCED</u>, which means <u>oxygen is removed</u> from it.

4) The carbon gains the oxygen and is <u>OXIDISED</u>, e.g.

> iron(III) oxide   +   carbon   →   iron   +   carbon dioxide

> zinc oxide   +   carbon   →   zinc   +   carbon dioxide

> copper(II) oxide   +   carbon   →   copper   +   carbon dioxide

5) You can also use <u>balanced symbol equations</u> to show these reactions.
For example:

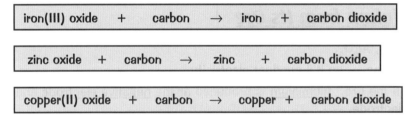

iron(III) oxide   +   carbon   →   iron   +   carbon dioxide
$$2Fe_2O_3(s)   +   3C(s)   →   4Fe(s)   +   3CO_2(g)$$

Flick back to page 28 for more on how to write out balanced equations and state symbols.

6) Don't forget what the different <u>state symbols</u> mean —
s = <u>solid</u>, g = <u>gas</u>, l = <u>liquid</u> and aq = <u>aqueous</u> (dissolved in water).

Metals are Extracted in Different Ways

1) Only metals that are <u>less reactive than carbon</u> can be extracted using <u>carbon</u>.

2) This is because the carbon can <u>reduce</u> the <u>metal oxide</u> and <u>take the oxygen</u> away from the metals.

3) Metals that are <u>more reactive</u> than carbon <u>can't</u> be extracted by reduction —
they have to be extracted by <u>electrolysis</u> (see next page).

Miners — they always have to stick their ore in...

Extracting metals isn't cheap. You have to pay for special equipment, energy and labour. Then there's the cost of getting the ore to the extraction plant. If there's a choice of extraction methods, a company always picks the <u>cheapest</u>, unless there's a good reason not to. Reduction with carbon is one of the cheaper ways.

Electrolysis

Electrolysis is a useful way of extracting <u>reactive metals</u> from their ores.

Electrolysis Means 'Splitting Up with Electricity'

1) You need to know this...

> <u>Electrolysis</u> is the <u>decomposition</u> (breaking down) of an electrolyte using <u>electricity</u>.

2) An <u>electrolyte</u> is a liquid that <u>conducts electricity</u>.

3) Electrolytes are usually <u>free ions dissolved in water</u> (e.g. <u>dissolved salts</u>) or <u>molten ionic compounds</u>.

NaCl dissolved
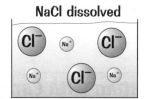

Molten NaCl
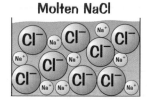

4) It's the <u>free ions</u> that <u>conduct</u> the electricity and allow the whole thing to work.

Electrolysis **Removes** Aluminium **from Its** Ore

1) Aluminium ore contains <u>aluminium oxide</u>, Al_2O_3.

2) <u>Molten</u> aluminium oxide contains <u>free ions</u> — so it'll <u>conduct electricity</u>.

3) The electric current is passed through the ore. <u>Aluminium</u> is produced at the <u>negative electrode</u> and <u>oxygen</u> is produced at the <u>positive electrode</u>.

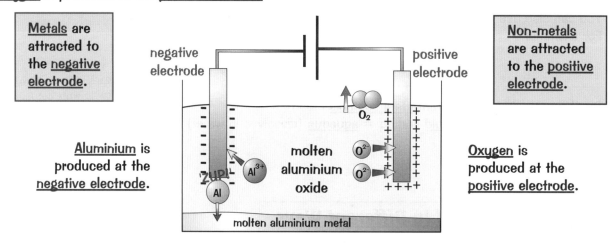

<u>Metals</u> are attracted to the <u>negative</u> electrode.	<u>Non-metals</u> are attracted to the <u>positive</u> electrode.

<u>Aluminium</u> is produced at the <u>negative electrode</u>.

<u>Oxygen</u> is produced at the <u>positive electrode</u>.

4) The equation for the decomposition of <u>aluminium oxide</u> is:

> aluminium oxide → aluminium + oxygen
> $$2Al_2O_{3(l)} \rightarrow 4Al_{(l)} + 3O_{2(g)}$$

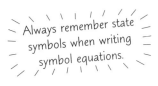

Always remember state symbols when writing symbol equations.

Faster shopping at Tesco — use Electrolleys...

Electrolysis ain't cheap — it takes a lot of <u>electricity</u>, which costs <u>money</u>. It's the only way of extracting some metals from their ores though, so it's <u>worth it</u>. Don't forget to have a go at drawing the diagram <u>from memory</u>.

Calculating Masses

You may be asked to calculate the mass of a metal in a certain mineral given its formula. But to do all that you'll need to understand relative atomic mass and relative formula mass. It's not as bad as it sounds...

Relative Atomic Mass, A_r — Easy Peasy

1) This is just a way of saying how heavy different atoms are.

2) You can find out an element's relative atomic mass by looking at the periodic table.

3) In the periodic table, the elements all have two numbers. The bigger one is the relative atomic mass.

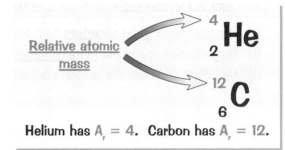

Helium has $A_r = 4$. Carbon has $A_r = 12$.

Relative Formula Mass, M_r — Also Easy Peasy

1) Compounds like $MgCl_2$ have a relative formula mass, M_r.

2) It's just all the relative atomic masses added together.

3) For example $MgCl_2$ would be:

$$MgCl_2$$
$$24 \quad + \quad (35.5 \times 2) \quad = \quad 95$$

So the M_r for $MgCl_2$ is simply 95.

Compounds with Brackets in...

1) Some compounds have brackets, for example magnesium hydroxide, $Mg(OH)_2$.

2) These are just as easy to work out.

3) The small number 2 after the bracket in the formula $Mg(OH)_2$ simply means that there's two of everything inside the brackets.

The brackets in the sum are in the same place as the brackets in the chemical formula.

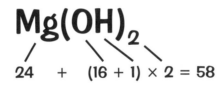

$$Mg(OH)_2$$
$$24 \quad + \quad (16 + 1) \times 2 = 58$$

So the relative formula mass for $Mg(OH)_2$ is 58.

Gram Formula Mass — Easy Peasy Squeezy Lemon

1) The gram formula mass is the same as the relative formula mass — but it has the units grams. For example the M_r of $MgCl_2$ is 95 — so the gram formula mass is 95 g.

2) You can work out the mass of an element in the gram formula mass of a compound. You just multiply its A_r by the number of atoms of the element, with the unit grams.

3) So the mass of Cl in $MgCl_2$ is $2 \times A_r = 2 \times 35.5 = 71$ g.

Numbers? — and you thought you were doing chemistry...

Learn the definitions of relative atomic mass and relative formula mass, then have a go at these:

1) * Use the periodic table to find the relative atomic mass of these elements: Cu, K, Kr, Cl

2) * Also find the relative formula mass of these compounds: NaOH, HNO_3, KCl, $CaCO_3$

48

Metals

Who'd have thought you'd find metals lurking about in rocks...
Now you've seen how to extract them, it's time to learn all about metals and their <u>properties</u>, yay...

Metal Properties are All Due to the Strong Metallic Bonds

1) <u>Metals</u> have a <u>giant structure</u> held together by strong bonds.
2) These bonds are called <u>metallic bonds</u>.
3) Metallic bonds are the reason why metals have certain <u>properties</u>.

1) Most Metals are Strong and Malleable

Metallic bonds mean metals are <u>strong</u> and <u>hard to break</u>.
They're also <u>malleable</u> — they can be <u>shaped</u>.

> Metals' strength and 'bendability' makes them handy for making into things like <u>bridges</u> and <u>car bodies</u>.

2) They Generally Have High Melting and Boiling Points

Metallic bonds are <u>very strong</u>, so it takes a lot of <u>energy</u> to break them.
This means metals have <u>high melting and boiling points</u>.

> Metals' high melting and boiling points make them handy — you don't want your <u>saucepan</u> to melt when you're cooking, or <u>bridges</u> to melt in hot weather.

3) Metals are Good Conductors of Heat and Electricity

Heat and electricity travel (are <u>conducted</u>) through metals really <u>easily</u>.

> Metals are ideal if you want to make something that heat needs to travel through, like a <u>saucepan base</u>.
> Their electrical conductivity makes them great for making things like <u>electrical wires</u>.

Don't try this at home. You'll die.

Someone robbed your metal? — call a copper...

The skin of the <u>Statue of Liberty</u> is made of copper — about 80 tonnes of it in fact. Its surface reacts with gases in the air to form <u>copper carbonate</u> — which is why it's that pretty shade of <u>green</u>. It was a present from France to the United States — I wonder if they found any wrapping paper big enough...

Module C5 — Chemicals of the Natural Environment

Environmental Impact of Metals

Metals are definitely a big part of modern life. Once they're finished with, it's far better to recycle them than to dig up more ore and extract fresh metal.

Ores are Finite Resources

1) Finite means that there's a limited amount — so eventually, the ore will run out.

2) People have to balance the advantages and disadvantages of mining the ores.

Advantages of mining	Disadvantages of mining
Produces metal which is used to make useful things.	Makes a mess of the landscape and destroys habitats for plants and animals.
Provides people with jobs.	Uses a lot of energy that is likely to be made by burning fossil fuels.
Brings money to the area which can be used to improve things like hospitals and transport.	A lot of pollution is produced by the increase in traffic.

Recycling Metals is Important

1) Mining and extracting metals takes lots of energy — which mostly comes from burning fossil fuels.

2) Recycling metals uses a lot less energy so less fossil fuels are burned.

3) Energy isn't cheap, so recycling saves money too.

4) There's a finite amount of each metal in the Earth, so recycling saves these resources.

5) Recycling metal means less rubbish gets sent to landfill. Landfill takes up space and pollutes the surroundings.

For example...

- If you didn't recycle aluminium, you'd have to mine more aluminium ore.

- But mining makes a mess of the landscape (and these mines are often in rainforests).

- The ore then needs to be transported, and the aluminium extracted (which uses loads of electricity).

- Recycling means you'll save the cost of sending your used aluminium to landfill.

- So for every bit of aluminium recycled you save loads of energy and a lot of waste — which sounds pretty good.

Recycling — do the Tour de France twice...

Recycling metal saves natural resources and money and reduces environmental problems. It's great. There's no limit to the number of times metals like aluminium, copper and steel can be recycled. So your humble little drink can may one day form part of a powerful robot who takes over the galaxy.

Revision Summary for Module C5

Here are some questions for you to get your teeth into. Have a go at them. If there are any you can't do, go back to the section and do a bit more learning, then try again. It's not fun, but it's the best way to make sure you know everything. Hop to it.

1) Name a gas in air that is a compound. Give the formula of this gas.

2) Explain why most molecular substances are gases.

3) What sort of bond joins the atoms in a molecular substance?

4)* Ethane can be represented by the 2-D diagram $\begin{array}{c} H \ H \\ | \ \ | \\ H-C-C-H \\ | \ \ | \\ H \ H \end{array}$ Write down its molecular formula.

5) Do solid ionic compounds have low or high boiling points? Explain why.

6) Why can ionic compounds conduct electricity when dissolved in water but not when they're solid?

7) A student makes a solution of an unknown compound. She adds a couple of drops of sodium hydroxide. She gets a white precipitate. She adds more sodium hydroxide and the precipitate dissolves. Use the table to work out which positive ion is present.

"Metal"	Colour of precipitate
Calcium, Ca^{2+}	White
Copper(II), Cu^{2+}	Blue
Iron(II), Fe^{2+}	Sludgy green
Iron(III), Fe^{3+}	Reddish brown
Zinc, Zn^{2+}	White at first. If more sodium hydroxide is added it redissolves to form a colourless solution.

8) What's the test for carbon dioxide?

9) Silver nitrate is added to a solution to test for negative ions. A cream precipitate forms. Using this table, work out what the negative ion in solution is.

Solution	Negative Ion	Precipitate
barium chloride solution	sulfate ion (SO_4^{2-})	white precipitate
silver nitrate solution	chloride ion (Cl^-)	white precipitate
	bromide ion (Br^-)	cream precipitate
	iodide ion (I^-)	yellow precipitate

10) What is the Earth's lithosphere?

11) Diamonds are used in drill tips and cutting tools because they're really hard. Explain how the bonding in diamond gives it this physical property.

12) What is a metal ore?

13) Carbon can be used to extract metal from its ore. Does the metal have to be more or less reactive than carbon for this method to work?

14) What is an electrolyte?

15)* Find A_r or M_r for each of these (use the periodic table):
a) Ca   b) Ag   c) CO_2 d) $MgCO_3$ e) $Al(OH)_3$ f) Na_2CO_3

16)* Find:
a) the gram formula mass of MgO   b) the mass of Fe in the gram formula mass of Fe_2O_3.

17) Why have metals got high melting and boiling points?

18) Give one impact on the environment for each of the following:
a) extracting metals,
b) disposing of metals.

The Chemical Industry

Chemical synthesis is making complicated chemical compounds from simple ones.
That's what this section is all about. It's going to be thrilling...

The Chemical Industry Makes Useful Products

Loads of chemicals in day-to-day life are made by chemical synthesis. Here are a few examples...

1) Food additives — these are used to help preserve, colour and flavour food.

2) Decorating products — things like paints contain loads of different pigments and dyes.

3) Drugs — the pharmaceutical industry makes all the medicines for helping you get over headaches or upset tummies.

4) Fertilisers — are used to help crops grow.

The Chemical Industry is Huge

It's absolutely massive. It makes tonnes and tonnes of chemicals and loads and loads of money.

Chemicals can be produced on a large or small scale.

1) Some chemicals are produced on a massive scale — lots and lots and lots of them are made.

2) Other chemicals are produced on a smaller scale — only small amounts of them are made.

There are loads of different sectors within the chemical industry.

1) The chemical industry is made up of lots of different sectors which make different types of chemical.

2) You might have to interpret data on the different sectors in the chemical industry.

3) For example, looking at the pie chart on the right:
   - the pharmaceutical industry has the largest share of the industry — it's 37%.
   - plastic and rubber make up 8%.
   - agrochemicals (chemicals used in farming) only make up 3% of the total chemical industry.

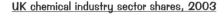

UK chemical industry sector shares, 2003

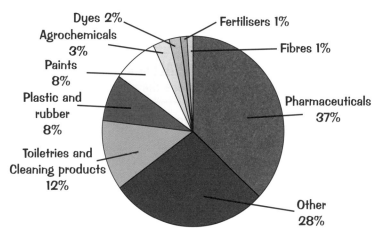

You'd need a big fish to make all those chemicals on a scale...

You don't need to remember all the figures on the pie chart but they may ask you to interpret a similar one in the exam. Don't worry though — everything you'll need to answer the questions will be there.

Acids and Alkalis

You'll find <u>acids</u> and <u>alkalis</u> at <u>home</u>, in the <u>lab</u> and in <u>industry</u> — they're an important set of chemicals.

Substances can be Acidic, Alkaline or Neutral

The <u>pH scale</u> goes from a very strong <u>acid</u> (pH 0) to a very strong <u>alkali</u> (pH 14).

These are the colours you get when you add universal indicator to an acid or an alkali.

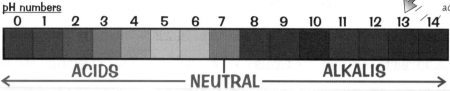

pH numbers
0 1 2 3 4 5 6 7 8 9 10 11 12 13 14

←———— ACIDS ————— NEUTRAL ———— ALKALIS ————→

Pure acidic compounds can be:

- <u>solids</u> (e.g. <u>citric acid</u>, and <u>tartaric acid</u>)

- <u>liquids</u> (e.g. <u>sulfuric acid</u>, <u>nitric acid</u> and <u>ethanoic acid</u>)

- <u>gases</u> (e.g. <u>hydrogen chloride</u>).

Common alkalis include <u>sodium hydroxide</u>, <u>potassium hydroxide</u> and <u>calcium hydroxide</u>.

Indicators and pH Meters can be Used to Measure pH

1) Indicators <u>change colour</u> depending on the pH.

2) <u>Litmus paper</u> turns <u>red</u> if the solution is <u>acidic</u> and <u>blue</u> if it's <u>alkaline</u>.

3) <u>Universal indicator</u> gives the colours shown above.

4) <u>pH meters</u> give a <u>reading</u> of the pH.

Reactions Between Acids and Alkalis Make Salts

An <u>ACID</u> is a substance with a pH of less than 7.
When acidic compounds are dissolved in <u>water</u> they produce <u>aqueous hydrogen ions</u>, <u>H^+</u>(aq).

An <u>ALKALI</u> is a substance with a pH of greater than 7.
When alkaline compounds are dissolved in <u>water</u> they produce <u>aqueous hydroxide ions</u>, <u>OH^-</u>(aq).

1) An acid and an alkali <u>react together</u> to form a <u>salt</u> and <u>water</u>.

2) This is called a <u>neutralisation reaction</u>.

3) Here's the equation:

$$acid + alkali \rightarrow salt + water$$

4) You can also show a neutralisation as a <u>symbol equation</u>.

5) The <u>H^+</u> ions from the <u>acid</u> react with the <u>OH^-</u> ions from the <u>alkali</u> to make <u>water</u>.

$$H^+_{(aq)} + OH^-_{(aq)} \rightarrow H_2O_{(l)}$$

All my indicators are orange...

There's no getting away from acids and alkalis in Chemistry, or even in real life. They're everywhere — acids are found in loads of <u>foods</u>, either naturally like in fruit, or as <u>flavourings</u> and <u>additives</u>. Alkalis (particularly sodium hydroxide) are used to help make all sorts of things from <u>soaps</u> to <u>posh plates</u>.

Module C6 — Chemical Synthesis

Acids Reacting with Metals

When you add a <u>metal</u> to an <u>acid</u> you get a <u>salt</u> and <u>hydrogen</u>. And this is a lovely equation showing it...

Acid + Metal → Salt + Hydrogen

It's written big 'cos it's kinda worth remembering. Here's the <u>typical experiment</u>:

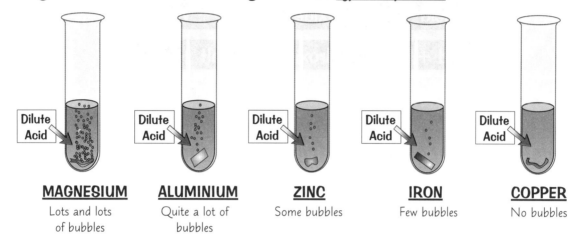

MAGNESIUM	ALUMINIUM	ZINC	IRON	COPPER
Lots and lots of bubbles	Quite a lot of bubbles	Some bubbles	Few bubbles	No bubbles

1) The more <u>reactive</u> the metal, the <u>faster</u> the reaction will go and the <u>more bubbles</u> there will be.

2) The <u>bubbles</u> are the <u>hydrogen gas</u> that's given off.

3) The <u>name</u> of the <u>salt</u> produced depends on which <u>metal</u> is used, and which <u>acid</u> is used.

Hydrochloric Acid Will Always Produce Chloride Salts:

hydrochloric acid + magnesium → magnesium chloride + hydrogen
hydrochloric acid + aluminium → aluminium chloride + hydrogen
hydrochloric acid + zinc → zinc chloride + hydrogen

Sulfuric Acid Will Always Produce Sulfate Salts:

sulfuric acid + magnesium → magnesium sulfate + hydrogen
sulfuric acid + aluminium → aluminium sulfate + hydrogen
sulfuric acid + zinc → zinc sulfate + hydrogen

Symbol Equations can Show the Reaction Between Metals and Salts

1) You can also show these reactions using <u>balanced symbol equations</u>. For example:

hydrochloric acid + magnesium → magnesium chloride + hydrogen
$$2HCl(l) + 2Mg(s) → 2MgCl(aq) + H_2(g)$$

There's more on symbol equations and state symbols on p.28.

2) A balanced symbol equation shows you the number of <u>molecules</u> or <u>atoms</u> of reactant <u>taking part</u> in the reaction.

3) Don't forget the <u>state symbols</u> — l = <u>liquid</u>, s = <u>solid</u>, g = <u>gas</u> and aq = <u>aqueous</u> (dissolved in <u>water</u>).

<u>What's in a name? — the acid and metal that made the salt apparently...</u>

Make sure you learn that big equation at the top of the page and then try writing equations for <u>different combinations</u> of <u>acids</u> and <u>metals</u>. Cover the page and scribble all the equations down. If you make any mistakes just try again...

Oxides, Hydroxides and Carbonates

Here's more stuff on <u>neutralisation</u> reactions — mixing <u>acids</u> with <u>oxides</u>, <u>hydroxides</u> and <u>carbonates</u>.

Metal Oxides and Metal Hydroxides React with Acids

All metal oxides and hydroxides <u>react with acids</u> to form <u>a salt</u> and <u>water</u>.

Acid + Metal Oxide → Salt + Water

Acid + Metal Hydroxide → Salt + Water

These are neutralisation reactions.

The Combination of Metal and Acid Decides the Salt

1) You might have to work out the <u>name</u> of the <u>salt</u> produced when an acid and metal react.

2) First, look for the <u>name of the metal</u>, e.g. copper or sodium — that'll be the metal in the salt.

3) Then look at the <u>type of acid</u> — hydrochloric acid produces <u>chlorides</u> and sulfuric acid produces <u>sulfates</u>.

4) Here are a couple of examples of <u>metal oxides</u> reacting with acids:

> hydrochloric acid   +   copper oxide   →   copper chloride   +   water
>
> sulfuric acid   +   zinc oxide   →   zinc sulfate   +   water

5) And here are a couple of examples of <u>metal hydroxides</u> reacting with acids:

> hydrochloric acid   +   sodium hydroxide   →   sodium chloride   +   water
>
> sulfuric acid   +   calcium hydroxide   →   calcium sulfate   +   water

Metal Carbonates Give Salt + Water + Carbon Dioxide

More gripping reactions involving acids. At least there are some <u>bubbles</u> involved here.

Acid + Metal Carbonate → Salt + Water + Carbon Dioxide

1) The reaction is the same as any other neutralisation reaction EXCEPT that <u>carbonates</u> give off <u>carbon dioxide</u> as well.

2) <u>Practise</u> writing the following equations out <u>from memory</u> — it'll do you no harm at all.

> hydrochloric acid + sodium carbonate → sodium chloride + water + carbon dioxide
>
> hydrochloric acid + calcium carbonate → calcium chloride + water + carbon dioxide

Someone threw some sodium chloride at me — I said, "Hey that's a salt"...

Working out the names of <u>salts</u> can be tricky. Make sure you read the examples <u>carefully</u> so you can see where each bit comes from. Then it doesn't matter what reaction they give you, you'll be able to work it out. Once you can do it for all the examples on the page tap the ends of your fingers and repeat after me... <u>excellent</u>.

Synthesising Compounds

When it comes to <u>making</u> chemicals it's not just a case of throwing everything into a bucket. Oh no, there are quite a few <u>stages</u> to the <u>process</u> — <u>six</u>, to be precise.

There are Six Stages Involved in Chemical Synthesis

① CHOOSING THE REACTION

Chemists need to choose the reaction (or series of reactions) to make the product. E.g. if they want to make a <u>salt</u> they might use a <u>neutralisation</u> reaction.

② RISK ASSESSMENT

1) This is an assessment of anything in the process that could <u>cause injury</u>.

2) It involves spotting possible <u>hazards</u> and then working out ways to <u>reduce the risk</u> of them harming someone.

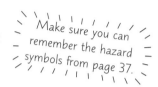

Make sure you can remember the hazard symbols from page 37.

③ CHOOSING THE APPARATUS AND CONDITIONS

1) The reaction needs to be carried out using suitable <u>apparatus</u> (equipment) and in the right <u>conditions</u>.

2) For example, the apparatus needs to be the <u>right size</u> (for the <u>amount</u> of product and reactants).

3) Chemists need to decide on the <u>temperature</u> and the <u>concentration of reactants</u>.

④ SEPARATING THE PRODUCT OUT

1) After the reaction is finished the products may need to be separated from the <u>reaction mixture</u>.

2) <u>Filtration</u> is used to separate <u>solids</u> from a <u>liquid</u> reaction mixture.

Filter paper folded into a cone shape — the solid is left in the filter paper.

⑤ PURIFICATION

1) <u>Purification</u> means <u>removing unwanted substances</u> so you are just left with the product you want.

2) <u>Evaporation</u> and <u>crystallisation</u> are used to separate a <u>soluble solid from solution</u>.

3) <u>Drying</u> is used to <u>remove water</u>. It can be done in an <u>oven</u> or a <u>desiccator</u>.

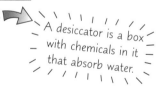

A desiccator is a box with chemicals in it that absorb water.

4) Purifying a product is a really <u>important</u> step in the chemical industry because the <u>impurities</u> might cause <u>problems</u>. E.g. impurities in medicines might do more harm than good.

⑥ MEASURING YIELD AND PURITY

1) The <u>yield</u> is <u>how much product</u> you get at the end of the reaction.

2) The <u>purity</u> of the chemical also needs to be measured — you can do this using <u>titration</u>.

Exams — definitely a hazard. Learn this page to reduce risk of harm...

So, six stages to making chemicals. It's important that none of them are <u>missed out</u>. It'd be pointless if you couldn't <u>separate</u> the product from the <u>reaction mixture</u>, and even worse if the process caused <u>injury</u> or <u>death</u>.

Calculating Masses in Reactions

When you're making chemicals it's always useful to know how much of the reactants you'll need or how much product you'll get. To do this you'll need to be able to work out <u>relative formula masses</u> from <u>relative atomic masses</u>. You've done this before on page 47, but here's a quick reminder.

Relative Atomic Masses are used to Work Out Relative Formula Masses

1) Relative atomic masses show the mass of an atom of one element <u>compared</u> to the mass of an atom of other elements.

2) The <u>relative atomic mass</u> (A_r) of an element is the <u>top number</u> when you look at the periodic table.

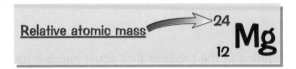

Relative atomic mass → $^{24}_{12}Mg$

3) To work out the <u>relative formula mass</u> (M_r) of a compound you <u>add up the A_r</u> of all the atoms in it.

4) For example, to work out the M_r of <u>sodium hydroxide</u> (<u>NaOH</u>):

> The A_r of Na = 23, A_r of O = 16 and A_r of H = 1.
> So the M_r of NaOH is 23 + 16 + 1 = <u>40</u>

Calculating Masses from Relative Formula Masses

You might have to work out <u>how much</u> of something reacts —
that's when you need the <u>relative formula mass</u> of a compound

<u>Example:</u> Calculate the <u>mass of magnesium</u> (Mg) needed to produce 100 g of magnesium oxide (MgO). Use the equation and formula below.

> <u>Equation:</u> $2Mg + O_2 \rightarrow 2MgO$
>
> <u>Formula:</u> mass of Mg = $\dfrac{M_r \text{ of Mg}}{M_r \text{ of MgO}} \times$ mass of MgO

Don't worry if the formula looks slightly different — you just have to put the right numbers in the right place to get the answer.

<u>Answer:</u> **Step 1:** To work out the mass of Mg using the formula you need to know the M_rs of Mg and MgO.

So, work out the <u>relative formula masses</u>:

- Magnesium: Mg = <u>24</u>
- Magnesium oxide: (Mg + O) = (24 + 16) = <u>40</u>

This was given to you in the question.

Step 2: Then put the numbers into the <u>formula</u>:

> mass of Mg = $\dfrac{M_r \text{ of Mg}}{M_r \text{ of MgO}} \times$ mass of MgO $= \dfrac{24}{40} \times 100 \text{ g} = $ <u>60 g</u>

Reaction mass calculations — no worries, matey...

The only way to get good at these is to <u>practise</u>. So make sure you can do the example, then try this one:
1)* Calcium reacts with oxygen to make calcium oxide. What mass of calcium (Ca) gives 30 g of calcium oxide (CaO)?

Equation: $2Ca + O_2 \rightarrow 2CaO$ Formula: mass of Ca = $\dfrac{M_r \text{ of Ca}}{M_r \text{ of CaO}} \times$ mass of CaO

Measuring Yield

You need to understand the <u>difference</u> between the <u>actual yield</u>, the <u>theoretical yield</u> and the <u>percentage yield</u> of a product. I know it's not the most fun thing to learn — but if it's in the exam you'll be glad you have.

Actual Yield *is What You Got*

1) The <u>ACTUAL YIELD</u> is the <u>mass</u> of <u>pure</u>, <u>dry product</u> you get at the end of the process.

2) You can work out the actual yield by <u>weighing the dried product</u>.

Theoretical Yield *is What You Think You Should Have Got*

1) The <u>THEORETICAL YIELD</u> is the <u>maximum amount</u> of pure product that <u>could</u> have been made.

2) You can work it out from the <u>balanced symbol equation</u> and <u>relative formula masses</u> (using the maths you learnt on the previous page).

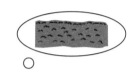

Percentage Yield *Compares* Actual *and* Theoretical *Yield*

1) The <u>PERCENTAGE YIELD</u> is the <u>actual yield</u> of the product as a <u>percentage</u> of the <u>theoretical yield</u>.

2) You can work it out using this formula:

$$\text{percentage yield} = \frac{\text{actual yield (grams)}}{\text{theoretical yield (grams)}} \times 100$$

3) The percentage yield will <u>always be less than 100%</u> — so if you do a calculation and get an answer of 135% you know it's gone wrong somewhere.

Example David reacts <u>sodium hydroxide</u> and <u>hydrochloric acid</u> to make sodium chloride.
The <u>actual yield</u> for the experiment was 79.2 g.
The <u>theoretical yield</u> for the experiment was 90 g.
Calculate the <u>percentage yield</u> for the experiment.

Answer $\text{percentage yield} = \dfrac{\text{actual yield (grams)}}{\text{theoretical yield (grams)}} \times 100 = \dfrac{79.2}{90} \times 100 = \underline{88\%}$

It can all be quite dull — like watching chemicals dry...

No matter how hard you try, you can't get a 100% yield in any reaction. You <u>always</u> lose a little bit of product. Make sure you don't lose any of the information on this page by covering it up and scribbling it all out again.

Titrations

Titrations have a bad reputation — but they're not as bad as they're made out to be.

Titrations are Carried Out Using a Burette

Titrations are a really handy type of experiment — see the next page for what they're used for.
For now you just need to know how to do them:

1) Measure some <u>alkali</u> into a <u>titration flask</u>.

2) Then add two or three drops of <u>indicator</u>.

3) Fill a <u>burette</u> with an acid — then take a reading by writing down <u>how much acid</u> is in the burette.

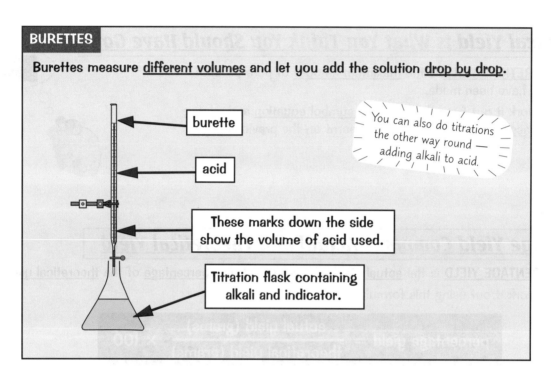

BURETTES

Burettes measure <u>different volumes</u> and let you add the solution <u>drop by drop</u>.

burette

acid

These marks down the side show the volume of acid used.

Titration flask containing alkali and indicator.

You can also do titrations the other way round — adding alkali to acid.

4) Using the <u>burette</u>, add the <u>acid</u> to the alkali a bit at a time.

5) Keep giving the titration flask a <u>swirl</u> to help <u>mix</u> the solutions.

- The <u>end point</u> of the titration is when <u>all</u> the alkali has been <u>neutralised</u> by the acid.

- This will cause the indicator in the flask to <u>chang colour</u>.

6) You need to go <u>slow</u> when you think the <u>end point</u> is about to be reached.

7) When you reach the end point and the indicator changes colour <u>stop</u> adding the acid.

8) Then <u>write down</u> the <u>final volume</u> of acid in the burette.

9) You can work out the <u>volume of acid</u> used to neutralise the alkali by calculating the <u>difference</u> between the <u>first</u> and <u>final</u> reading of the burette.

Acids are always in trouble — they just keep getting dropped in it...

Titrations aren't too tricky really — you just need to make sure your results are <u>accurate</u>, which means <u>going slowly near the end-point</u>. Oh, and don't forget the indicator — you'll be waiting a long time without it.

More on Titrations

These titrations are useful things. Ok, so it might not seem that way right now but by the end of the page you'll see that they can be used to find out the concentration of a solution and that's very useful — honest.

Solids are Dissolved Before Being Used in a Titration

1) Titrations can't be carried out with solids — only liquids.

2) So any solid alkali or acid being tested needs to be made into a solution.

Method
- Crush the solid into a powder.
- Put a flask onto some scales.
- Carefully weigh some of the powdered solid into the flask.
- Add a solvent, e.g. water or ethanol, to dissolve the powder.
- Finally, swirl the titration flask until all of the solid has dissolved. Simple.

3) Once you've done this you can do the titration in the normal way (see previous page).

Titrations Can be Used to Work Out Concentrations

You can work out the concentration of a solution using the data from a titration.

Example — Working out the concentration of a sodium hydroxide solution.

Gordon wants to know the concentration of 0.025 dm^3 of sodium hydroxide (NaOH).

He does a titration using hydrochloric acid (HCl) and finds that it takes 0.01 dm^3 to neutralise the sodium hydroxide solution.

The concentration of the HCl is 4 g/dm^3.

Use the formula below to calculate the concentration of the sodium hydroxide solution.

$$\text{concentration of NaOH solution} = \frac{\text{concentration of HCl} \times \text{volume of HCl}}{\text{volume of NaOH solution}}$$

Answer

All you have to do is stick the numbers into the formula in the right places.

- Concentration of hydrochloric acid = 4 g/dm^3
- Volume of hydrochloric acid = 0.01 dm^3
- Volume of sodium hydroxide = 0.025 dm^3

$$\text{concentration of NaOH solution} = \frac{4 \times 0.01}{0.025} = \underline{1.6 \text{ g/dm}^3}$$

Concentrate when doing titrations...

This is all pretty complicated stuff, but don't worry about it too much. If you get asked to do it in the exam they'll give you all the information you need — like the formulas, concentrations and volumes.

Energy Transfer in Reactions

Whenever chemical reactions occur, there are changes in <u>energy</u>. Altogether now... oooo^{ooooo}ooo

Reactions are <u>Exothermic</u> or <u>Endothermic</u>

1) An <u>EXOTHERMIC</u> reaction <u>gives out energy</u> to the surroundings.
2) This means the temperature of the reaction mixture will <u>increase</u>.
3) An <u>ENDOTHERMIC</u> reaction <u>takes in energy</u> from the surroundings.
4) This means the temperature of the reaction mixture will <u>decrease</u>.

Energy Level Diagrams <u>Show if a Reaction is</u> <u>Exothermic</u> or <u>Endothermic</u>

<u>Energy level diagrams</u> show the <u>energy levels</u> of the <u>reactants</u> and <u>products</u>.

1) This one shows an <u>exothermic reaction</u>.
2) The products are at a <u>lower energy</u> than the reactants.
3) The <u>difference in height</u> shows how much energy is <u>given out</u>.

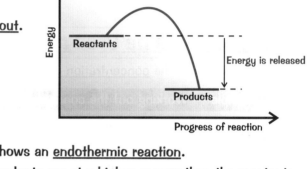

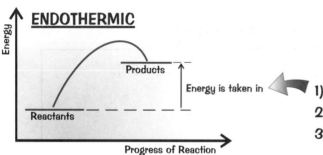

1) This shows an <u>endothermic reaction</u>.
2) The products are at a <u>higher energy</u> than the reactants.
3) The <u>difference in height</u> shows the <u>energy taken in</u>.

Energy Management <u>is Used to Control Reactions</u>

Scientists in the <u>chemical industry</u> need to know <u>how much energy</u> is taken in or given out during a reaction.

- If a chemical reaction is <u>exothermic</u> the <u>temperature</u> of the reaction mixture will <u>increase</u>.
- If the reaction mixture gets <u>too hot</u> then some of the reactants or products could become <u>gases</u>, which could cause an <u>explosion</u>.
- So the extra heat produced by the reaction has to be <u>removed</u>.

- If the reaction is <u>endothermic</u> the reaction mixture might become <u>too cold</u>.
- This could <u>slow down</u> the <u>rate of the reaction</u>, or the reaction mixture could <u>freeze</u>.
- This could <u>damage equipment</u> and stop the whole process.
- So the reaction mixture has to be <u>heated</u>.

Burning is exothermic and gives out heat — well I never...

Don't be put off by the long words here. Remember, "<u>exo-</u>" = <u>exit</u>, so an exothermic reaction is one that <u>gives out</u> heat. And "<u>endo-</u>" = erm... the other one. Okay, so there's no easy way to remember that one. Tough.

Rates of Reaction

There's an old saying in the chemical industry — the faster you make chemicals the faster you make money. So it's important to know what factors affect the rate of a chemical reaction.

Reactions Can Go at All Sorts of Different Rates

The rate of a reaction is how fast the reactants are changed into products.

1) Some reactions are slow, e.g. the rusting of iron.
2) Some reactions are fast, e.g. burning.
3) And some reactions are in the middle, e.g. a metal reacting with acid to give a gentle stream of bubbles.

Graphs Can be Used to Show Rates of Reaction

This graph shows the speed of a reaction under different conditions.

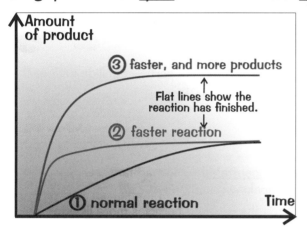

The fastest reactions have the steepest lines and become flat in the least time.

(1) Graph 1 shows the normal reaction.

(2) Graph 2 shows a faster reaction. You can tell it's faster because the line at the start is steeper.

(3) Graph 3 shows a reaction where more product is made. The line becomes flat at a higher amount of product.

It's also a faster reaction — the line is even steeper at the start.

Controlling the Rate of Reaction is Important in the Chemical Industry

1) In factories that make chemicals, it's important to control the rate of the reaction.
2) There are two main reasons:

- Safety — if the reaction is too fast it could cause an explosion, which can be dangerous.
- Economic (money) reasons — it's important the rate isn't too slow or the company won't make as much product and won't make as much money.

3) In the exam you might be given a load of info about different reactions and asked to pick the best one.
4) Look for reactions that will give the best yield (see p.57) and fastest rate for the lowest cost.
5) You'll also need to think about environmental issues (like poisonous gases) and how dangerous the reactions are.

Get a fast, furious reaction — tickle your teacher...

Make sure you understand what those graphs show. The lines that are steepest are the fastest. When they become flat the reaction has stopped and the height of the flat bit shows you how much product was formed.

More on Rates of Reaction

There are <u>four things</u> that affect rates of reaction. And you need to know about <u>all</u> of them. Yup, <u>all</u> four...

The Rate of Reaction Depends on Four Things:

LEARN THEM!

1) <u>TEMPERATURE</u> — <u>increasing</u> the temperature <u>increases</u> the rate of reaction.

2) <u>CONCENTRATION</u> — <u>increasing</u> the concentration <u>increases</u> the rate of reaction.

3) <u>CATALYST</u> — <u>using</u> a catalyst <u>increases</u> the rate of reaction.

4) <u>SIZE OF 'LUMPS'</u> (or surface area) — <u>smaller solid particles</u> (or more surface area) <u>increases</u> the rate of reaction.

More Collisions Increases the Rate of Reaction

<u>Reaction rates</u> are explained perfectly by <u>collision theory</u>. It's really simple.

1) The basic idea is that particles have to <u>collide</u> (hit each other) in order to <u>react</u>.

2) The <u>rate of a reaction</u> depends on the <u>collision frequency</u> — <u>how often</u> the particles <u>collide</u> with each other.

3) The collisions also need to have enough <u>energy</u> to cause a reaction or nothing will happen.

CONCENTRATION

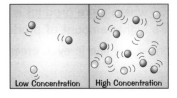

Low Concentration   High Concentration

1) If a solution is made more <u>concentrated</u> it means there are more particles of <u>reactant</u> knocking about.

2) This makes <u>collisions</u> between the reactant particles <u>more likely</u>.

SMALLER SOLID PARTICLES (or MORE SURFACE AREA)

1) If one of the reactants is a <u>solid</u> then <u>breaking it up</u> into <u>smaller</u> pieces will <u>increase its surface area</u>.

2) This means the particles around it will have <u>more area to work on</u>, so they'll <u>collide more often</u> and it'll be a faster reaction.

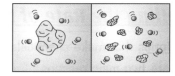

Catalysts Don't get Used Up

1) A <u>catalyst</u> is something that increases the <u>speed of a reaction</u>.

2) But it <u>doesn't</u> get used up in the reaction.

Collision theory — it's always the other driver...

Two particles bumping into each other isn't enough to cause a reaction — they have to have enough <u>energy</u> too. But if you <u>increase</u> the number of times the particles bump into each other (by increasing the <u>concentration</u> or <u>surface area</u>) then there's a much better chance of a reaction and that means a faster rate.

Measuring Rates of Reaction

All this talk about rates of reactions is fine and dandy, but it's no good if you can't measure it.

Three Ways to Measure the Speed of a Reaction

1) You can follow how <u>fast</u> a reaction is going by looking at how quickly the <u>reactants are used up</u> or how quickly the <u>products are made</u>.

2) The <u>faster</u> the reactants are used up or the <u>faster</u> the products are made the <u>faster the reaction</u> is.

3) You can <u>calculate</u> the speed (or <u>rate</u>) of a reaction using this equation:

> Rate of Reaction = $\dfrac{\text{Amount of reactant used or amount of product formed}}{\text{Time}}$

4) There are different ways that the speed of a reaction can be <u>measured</u>. Read on...

1) Precipitation and Colour Change

1) If the reactants are <u>see-through</u> and the product is a <u>precipitate</u> the solution will go <u>cloudy</u>.

2) If you put a <u>mark</u> behind the flask you can <u>time how long</u> it takes for the mark to <u>disappear</u>.

3) If the reactants are <u>coloured</u> and the products are <u>colourless</u>, you can time how long it takes for the solution to <u>lose its colour</u>.

4) If the reactants are <u>colourless</u> and the products are <u>coloured</u>, you can time how long it takes for the solution to <u>become coloured</u>.

5) The <u>faster</u> the mark or the colour <u>disappears</u>, the <u>quicker</u> the reaction.

Cloudy

2) Change in Mass (Usually Gas Given Off)

1) You can measure the speed of a reaction that <u>produces a gas</u> using a <u>balance</u>.

2) Just put the <u>flask</u> the reaction mixture is in on the balance.

3) As the gas is given off the <u>mass will drop</u>.

4) The <u>quicker</u> the reading on the balance <u>drops</u>, the <u>faster</u> the reaction.

3) The Volume of Gas Given Off

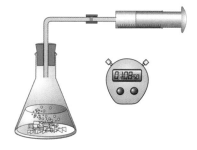

1) You can use a <u>gas syringe</u> to measure the <u>volume</u> of gas given off.

2) The <u>more</u> gas given off in a set amount of <u>time</u>, the <u>faster</u> the reaction.

OK, have you got your stopwatch ready... *BANG!* — oh...

You have to be quite careful with the gas syringe method — if the reaction is <u>too fast</u>, you can <u>blow the plunger</u> out of the end of the syringe. Wooo... The <u>balance</u> and the <u>gas syringe</u> are both quite <u>accurate</u>. The first method isn't that accurate, but if you're not producing a gas you can't use the other two. Ah well.

Module C6 — Chemical Synthesis

Revision Summary for Module C6

And that's it... the end of another section. Which means it's time for some more questions. There's no point in trying to duck out of these — they're the best way of testing that you've learned everything in this topic. If you can't answer any of them, look back in the book. If you can't do all this now, you won't be able to in the exam either.

1) Name two chemicals that you might come across in everyday life.

2) State whether substances with the following pH are acid, alkali or neutral:
   a) pH 2   b) pH 13   c) pH 0   d) pH 7

3) Give an example of an acidic compound that is a liquid.

4) Name two ways of measuring the pH of a substance.

5) What type of ion is produced when:
   a) an acid is dissolved in water?
   b) an alkali is dissolved in water?

6) Write the word equation for a neutralisation reaction.

7) Write word equations for the following reactions:
   a) hydrochloric acid reacting with magnesium.
   b) sulfuric acid reacting with aluminium.

8) Name the salts formed and write a balanced equation for the reaction between:
   a) hydrochloric acid and copper oxide.
   b) hydrochloric acid and calcium hydroxide.

9) What is a risk assessment?

10) How would you separate a solid product from a liquid reaction mixture?

11) Give two methods used to dry a product.

12)* What mass of magnesium oxide (MgO) is produced when 108 g of magnesium burns in air?

   Formula: $\text{mass of MgO} = \dfrac{M_r \text{ of MgO}}{M_r \text{ of Mg}} \times \text{mass of Mg}$

13)* Calculate the percentage yield of an experiment if the actual yield is 47 g and the theoretical yield is 50 g.

14) Describe how to carry out a titration.

15) Describe the method used to turn a solid into a solution for a titration.

16) What term is used to describe a reaction where energy is given out?

17) What term is used to describe a reaction where energy is taken in?

18) Draw energy level diagrams for the types of reaction you named in question 16 and 17.

19) Give two reasons why it is important to control the rate of a chemical reaction in industry.

20) What four things affect the rate of a reaction?

21) Describe three different ways of measuring the rate of a reaction.

Speed

This whole speed thing's pretty easy really. Just make sure you get lots of practice at <u>using the formula</u>.

Speed <u>is</u> Just the <u>Distance</u> Travelled in a Certain <u>Time</u>

1) To find the <u>speed</u> of an object (in <u>metres per second</u>, <u>m/s</u>), you need to know the <u>distance</u> it travels (in <u>metres</u>) and the <u>time</u> it takes (in <u>seconds</u>).

2) Practise using this <u>very easy formula</u>:

$$\text{Speed (m/s)} = \frac{\text{Distance travelled (m)}}{\text{Time taken (s)}}$$

<u>EXAMPLE 1</u>:   A cat creeps 20 metres in 40 seconds. Find its speed.

<u>ANSWER</u>:   speed = distance ÷ time = 20 ÷ 40 = <u>**0.5 m/s**</u>

<u>EXAMPLE 2</u>:   The cat sees a dog and legs it.
It now runs 20 metres in 25 seconds. Find its new speed.

<u>ANSWER</u>:   speed = distance ÷ time = 20 ÷ 25 = <u>**0.8 m/s**</u>

The <u>Speed</u> of an Object <u>Normally Changes</u>

1) In real life, it's <u>pretty rare</u> for an object to go at <u>exactly</u> the same speed for a <u>long time</u>.

2) So it's usually more <u>useful</u> to know the <u>average</u> speed.

3) This is what the <u>speed formula</u> will normally tell you.
For example, the cat had an <u>average</u> speed of 0.5 m/s in Example 1 above.

<u>EXAMPLE 3</u>:   A very fast sprinter can run 100 m in 9.8 seconds.
Find their average speed.

<u>ANSWER</u>:   speed = distance ÷ time = 100 ÷ 9.8 = <u>**10.2 m/s**</u>

4) Sometimes, it's handy to know something's <u>instantaneous</u> speed.

5) The instantaneous speed is the speed of an object at a <u>single point in time</u>.

6) To find this you just find the <u>average</u> speed over a very <u>small amount of time</u>.

Don't speed through this page — learn it properly...

Calculating speed is <u>easy</u> — you know the units are <u>m/s</u>, so you have to do <u>metres ÷ seconds</u>. This stuff is also quite useful in real life... Like if you want to know how fast you're going when you're running back to your house through the rain because you've left your phone inside. Not that I've ever done that...

Speed, Distance and Velocity

One way to look at the movement of an object is to draw a lovely old distance-time graph...

Distance-Time Graphs

In the exam you could be asked to draw a distance-time graph for a moving object, or make sense of one.

Very Important Notes:

1) GRADIENT = SPEED.

2) The steeper the gradient, the faster it's going.

3) Flat sections are where it's stationary (stopped).

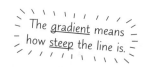
The gradient means how steep the line is.

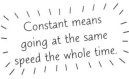
Constant means going at the same speed the whole time.

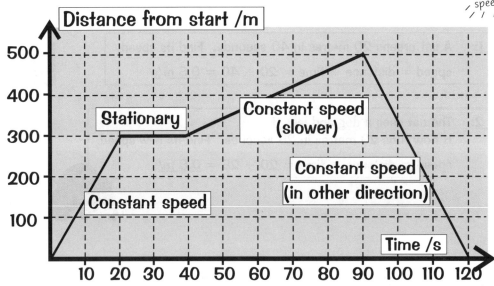

Distance from start /m

- Stationary
- Constant speed
- Constant speed (slower)
- Constant speed (in other direction)

Time /s

Speed is Just a Number, but Velocity Has Direction Too

1) The speed of an object is just how fast it's going — the direction isn't important.

   EXAMPLE: The bear was running at a speed of 30 m/s.

2) Velocity tells you the speed and direction.

   EXAMPLE: The bear was running at 30 m/s in the direction of terrified tourists.

3) Instantaneous velocity tells you the speed and direction at a single point in time.

4) So the instantaneous velocity is the instantaneous speed with a direction given.

Distance-time graphs — almost as fun as watching dried paint...

Distance-time graphs aren't exactly exciting, but you need to be really comfortable with what all the different lines mean. Have a go at sketching some for different journeys. You'll soon get the hang of it. Fun times.

Acceleration and Velocity

Acceleration is one of those topics that examiners just love. So make sure you learn this stuff dead well.

Acceleration is How Quickly You're Speeding Up

1) Acceleration is the change in velocity (or speed) in a certain amount of time.

2) Deceleration is just negative acceleration (slowing down).

3) If something slows down then the change in velocity will be negative.

4) Use this equation to work out acceleration:

$$\text{Acceleration (m/s}^2) = \frac{\text{Change in Velocity (m/s)}}{\text{Time Taken (s)}}$$

- First work out the "change in velocity".

- This is the final velocity minus the starting velocity (check out the example below).

- Notice that the units of acceleration are m/s².

If something is 'at rest' it means the velocity is 0 m/s.

EXAMPLE: A creeping cat speeds up from 2 m/s to 6 m/s in 5 s. Find its acceleration.

ANSWER: acceleration = change in velocity ÷ time taken = (6 – 2) ÷ 5 = 4 ÷ 5 = **0.8 m/s²**

Remember, if you get a negative acceleration don't panic. It just means the object is slowing down. Phew.

Speed-Time Graphs

You might be asked to draw a graph of speed against time, or to answer questions about a graph you're given.

Very Important Notes:

1) GRADIENT = ACCELERATION.

2) The steeper the gradient, the faster the acceleration.

3) A point at the origin (0,0), or any point where the graph touches the bottom axis, means the object is stationary (not moving).

4) Flat sections mean it's moving in a straight line at constant speed.

5) Uphill sections (/) are acceleration in a straight line.

6) Downhill sections (\) are deceleration in a straight line.

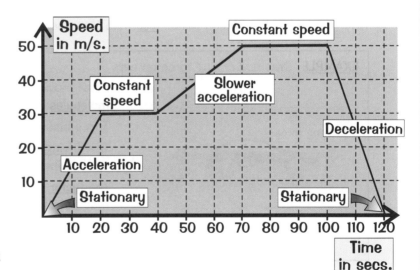

I can accelerate pretty quickly when there's food involved...

Hum di hum. Yes, I know the graph on this page looks a lot like the one on the previous page but they're most definitely not the same. This one shows how the speed changes with time. Make sure you triple check the labels on any graph you see in an exam. Those examiners can be tricksy and you don't want to be caught out.

Module P4 — Explaining Motion

Forces

A <u>force</u> is just a <u>push</u> or a <u>pull</u> and is measured in <u>Newtons</u> (<u>N</u>). Simple — or maybe not...

Forces Happen When Two Objects Interact

1) Forces come from two objects <u>interacting</u>.

2) When one <u>object</u> applies a <u>force</u> to the other, it always experiences a force <u>in return</u>.

3) These two forces are sometimes called an '<u>interaction pair</u>'.

4) For example, if <u>you push</u> against a <u>wall</u>, the <u>wall</u> will <u>push back</u> against <u>you</u> in the <u>opposite direction</u> with exactly the <u>same sized force</u>. And as soon as you <u>stop</u> pushing, <u>so does the wall</u>.

5) If you think about it, there must be an <u>opposing force</u> when you push against a wall — otherwise you (and the wall) would <u>fall over</u>.

6) The forces are the <u>same size</u> but they can still make things <u>move</u> because they act on <u>different objects</u>.

7) For example, a <u>jet engine</u> burns fuel to make <u>exhaust gases</u>. The jet engine <u>exerts a force</u> on the exhaust gases, making them <u>accelerate backwards</u>. The exhaust gases exert an equal but opposite force on the jet, making it <u>move forwards</u>.

8) The force on the gases and the force on the jet engine are an <u>interaction pair</u>.

Moving Objects Normally Experience Friction

1) When an object is trying to <u>move</u> against another one, both objects experience a <u>force</u>.

2) This force is called <u>friction</u>.

3) Friction acts in the <u>direction</u> that would <u>stop the object moving</u>.

4) The <u>frictional</u> force will <u>match</u> the size of the <u>force trying to move</u> the object, up to a <u>maximum point</u>.

5) After this point, the friction will be <u>less</u> than the other force and the object will <u>move</u>.

<u>EXAMPLE</u>: Drag and driving force on cars

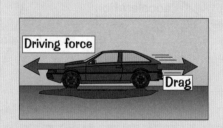

Driving force

Drag

- A car moving through air has to force its way <u>past</u> all the <u>molecules</u> in the air.
- This causes a type of <u>friction</u> which we call <u>drag</u>.
- The <u>driving force</u> (thrust) of a car has to push <u>against</u> the drag so that the car can move.
- The <u>faster</u> the car tries to go, the <u>bigger</u> the drag gets to try and <u>slow it down</u>.
- A <u>big, squarish</u> object like a lorry experiences <u>more</u> drag or <u>friction</u> than a <u>streamlined</u> object like a sports car.

Revision — what a drag...

An obvious joke, I know. But I can't be funny every day of my life — I'm no Steve Martin* you know. The stuff on this page may seem a bit crazy at first — but it'll get easier the more you look at it. Honest. You've got to <u>remember</u> that when something uses a <u>force</u> on an object, the object will give the same force <u>back</u>.

Forces

It's <u>all very well</u> knowing that there are forces acting <u>all over the place</u>,
but you need to be able to show <u>where</u> and <u>when</u> they're acting too...

Arrows *Show the Size* and *Direction* of Forces

1) You might be given a <u>diagram</u> of an <u>object</u> and asked to <u>draw arrows</u> showing the <u>forces acting on it</u>.

2) The <u>length</u> of the arrow shows the <u>size</u> of the force.

3) The <u>direction</u> of the arrow shows the <u>direction</u> of the force.

4) You might have to say <u>which object</u> the force is acting on.

5) If the arrows in <u>opposite pairs</u> are the same <u>size</u>, then the <u>forces</u> are <u>balanced</u>...

1) *The Reaction of a Surface* — Balanced **Forces**

1) An object <u>resting</u> on a surface pushes <u>downwards</u> (due to its weight).

2) The <u>surface</u> pushes upwards with an <u>equal and opposite force</u>.

3) This force is called the <u>reaction of the surface</u>.

4) The two forces are the <u>same size</u>, so the <u>arrows</u> are the same size.

5) The <u>heavier</u> the object, the <u>bigger</u> the reaction force gets to <u>match the weight</u> (up to a point).

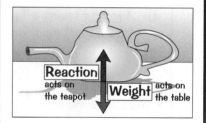

Reaction acts on the teapot | Weight acts on the table

2) *Steady Speed* — Balanced **Forces**

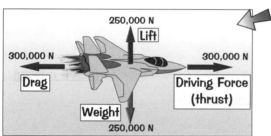

250,000 N Lift
300,000 N Drag
300,000 N Driving Force (thrust)
Weight 250,000 N

1) A jet <u>aircraft</u> is moving at a <u>steady speed</u> and at a <u>constant height</u>.

2) So the forces acting on it must be <u>balanced</u>.

3) The <u>drag</u> is <u>equal and opposite</u> to the force of the <u>driving force</u> produced by the engines.

4) The <u>lift</u> produced by air moving over the plane's <u>wings</u> is <u>equal and opposite</u> to the <u>weight</u> of the plane.

Resultant Force *is Really Important*

1) In many <u>real</u> situations, the forces acting on an object are <u>not</u> all the same size — they're <u>unbalanced</u>.

2) The <u>resultant force</u> is the <u>overall</u> force acting on an object.

3) This is the force you get when you <u>add up</u> all the <u>individual forces</u>, taking their <u>directions</u> into account.

4) Resultant force decides the <u>movement</u> of the object. ~Don't panic — resultant force is covered more on the next page.~

Resultant force... I'm pretty sure that's a Steven Seagal film...

Make sure you can tell what <u>object</u> a force is <u>acting on</u> and <u>how big</u> the force is. Just remember that the <u>length</u> of an arrow shows the <u>size</u> of the force. The <u>direction</u> is important too. <u>Revise</u> it well.

Forces and Momentum

"Not more forces!", I hear you scream... Don't worry my friend, this page has a <u>kangaroo</u> on it.

Acceleration — Un*balanced* Forces

1) Two forces acting on an object moving in a straight line are the <u>forwards driving force</u> and the <u>backwards counter force</u>.

2) If the <u>driving force</u> is <u>bigger</u> than the <u>counter force</u>, the object will <u>speed up</u>.

3) The <u>bigger</u> the difference, the <u>greater</u> the <u>acceleration</u>.

4) If the driving force is <u>less</u> than the counter force, the object <u>slows down</u>.

5) If the forces are <u>equal</u>, it moves at a <u>constant speed</u> in a <u>straight line</u>.

acceleration

Driving Force from engine

Counter Force from friction and air resistance

Example: forces acting on a <u>rocket</u>...

1) A <u>rocket</u> taking off <u>accelerates</u> away from the ground, so the <u>upward force</u> (the thrust) must be <u>greater</u> than the <u>downward forces</u> slowing it down.

2) In this case, there are <u>two downward forces</u> — <u>gravity</u> and <u>air resistance</u> (from <u>friction</u> between the rocket and the air).

↑ air resistance

3) If the thrust <u>stopped</u> (if the rocket ran out of fuel), then the downward forces would be <u>greater</u> than the upward forces. The rocket would <u>slow down</u> until it stopped and then <u>move downward</u>.

↓ gravity

4) The same ideas apply to things <u>thrown</u> up in the air then falling back to Earth.

thrust

gravity + air resistance

Momentum = Mass × Velocity

1) Momentum is mainly about how much '<u>oomph</u>' an object has — how hard it'd be to <u>stop it moving</u>.

2) The <u>greater</u> the <u>mass</u> or <u>velocity</u> of an object, the <u>more momentum</u> it has.

3) Momentum has size <u>and</u> direction (like <u>velocity</u>).

4) Here's a nice easy equation:

$$\text{Momentum} = \text{Mass} \times \text{Velocity}$$
$$\text{(kg m/s)} \qquad \text{(kg)} \qquad \text{(m/s)}$$

<u>EXAMPLE:</u> A <u>65 kg</u> kangaroo is moving in a straight line at <u>10 m/s</u>. Calculate its momentum.

<u>ANSWER:</u> Momentum = mass × velocity = 65 × 10 = 650 kg m/s

---

5) Momentum is affected by the <u>resultant force</u> acting on an object:

- A <u>resultant force</u> of <u>zero</u> means that a <u>stationary</u> object will <u>stay still</u>.

- A resultant force of <u>zero</u> means a <u>moving object</u> will carry on moving with the <u>same velocity</u> and <u>momentum</u>.

- A resultant force that's <u>not zero</u> means an object's <u>momentum changes</u> in the <u>direction of the force</u>.

Have a look at page 69 for more on resultant forces.

Accelerate your learning — force yourself to revise...

OK so there's another <u>equation of doom</u> for you to learn to use, but it's a fairly simple one. So get practising...

Forces and Momentum

Time to get your head around <u>changes in momentum</u>. A faster change = a greater chance of injury.

The Change in Momentum Depends on the Force

1) When a <u>resultant force</u> acts on an object, it causes a <u>change in momentum</u> in the direction of the force.

2) This change of momentum is <u>proportional</u> to the <u>size</u> of the force and the <u>time</u> it acts for:

$$\text{Change of momentum} = \text{Resultant force} \times \text{Time for which the force acts}$$
$$\text{(kg m/s)} \qquad\qquad \text{(N)} \qquad\qquad\qquad \text{(s)}$$

<u>EXAMPLE:</u> A comet hits a rock travelling through space. It gives the rock a resultant force of <u>2500 N</u> for <u>0.7 seconds</u>. Calculate the rock's <u>change in momentum</u>.

<u>ANSWER:</u> Change of momentum = force × time = 2500 × 0.7 = <u>1750 kg m/s</u>

3) So, the <u>bigger the force</u> and the <u>longer</u> it acts for, the <u>bigger</u> the <u>change in momentum</u>.

Car Safety Features Reduce Forces

1) If your momentum changes <u>very quickly</u>, the <u>forces</u> on your body will be very <u>large</u>.

2) Large forces are more likely to cause <u>injury</u>.

3) If your momentum changes <u>slowly</u> (like braking slowly in a car) the <u>forces</u> acting on your body are <u>small</u> and you're unlikely to be <u>hurt</u>.

4) In a <u>collision</u> (crash), you <u>can't change</u> the car's <u>mass</u> or its <u>change in velocity</u>. So the change in momentum stays <u>the same</u>.

5) But, you can <u>lower</u> the average <u>force</u> on an object by <u>slowing it down</u> over a <u>longer time</u>.

6) <u>Safety features</u> in a car <u>increase the collision time</u> to <u>reduce the forces</u> on the passengers:

<u>CRUMPLE ZONES</u> crumple on impact, <u>increasing the time</u> taken for the car to stop.

<u>AIR BAGS</u> also slow you down more <u>slowly</u>.

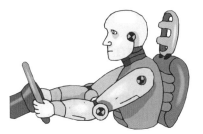

<u>SEAT BELTS</u> stretch slightly, <u>increasing the time</u> taken for the wearer to stop. This <u>reduces the forces</u> acting on the chest.

<u>CYCLE AND MOTORCYCLE HELMETS</u> provide padding that <u>increases the time</u> taken for your head to come to a stop if it <u>hits something hard</u>.

Learn this stuff — it'll only take a moment... um...

<u>Momentum</u>'s a pretty <u>important</u> bit of physics — so make sure you <u>learn it properly</u>. There are a few equations to cover in this section, but none of them are too hard, so keep <u>practising</u> different questions and Robert's your <u>mother's brother</u>. And never forget to stick the <u>units</u> on the end of your answers...

Work

In Physics, "work done" means something special. It's got its own formula and everything.

Work Done is Just Energy Transferred

When a force moves an object it does work and energy is transferred to the object.

1) When something moves, something else has to put in effort to move it.

2) The thing putting the effort in needs a supply of energy (like fuel or food or electricity).

3) It then does work by moving the object and transfers (changes) the energy it gets from fuel into other forms.

4) Whether this energy is transferred usefully (e.g. by lifting a load) or is wasted (e.g. lost as heat), you can still say that work is done.

5) Work done and energy transferred are both measured in joules (J).

> **Amount of energy transferred (J) = Work done (J)**

Work Done has a Formula

> **Work done by a force (J) = Force (N) × Distance moved in direction of force (m)**

This formula only works if the force is in exactly the same direction as the movement.

To find how much work has been done (in joules), you just multiply the force in newtons by the distance moved in metres. Easy as that. I'll show you...

> **EXAMPLE:** Some kids drag an old tractor tyre 5 m over flat ground. They pull with a total force of 340 N. Find the work done.
>
> **ANSWER:** work done = force × distance = 340 × 5 = 1700 J.

Revise work done — what else...

Have a go at using the formula in this question:
A gorilla finds himself with nothing to do on a Sunday evening, so he pushes a log 3 m across the forest floor using a force of 350 N. What is the work done by the gorilla on the log?*

Kinetic Energy

Work done always involves movement. That's where kinetic energy comes in...

Kinetic Energy *is Energy of Movement*

1) Anything that's moving has kinetic energy (K.E.).

2) The kinetic energy of an object depends on its mass and speed.

3) The greater its mass and the faster it's going, the bigger its kinetic energy.

4) There's a slightly tricky formula for it:

$$\text{Kinetic Energy} = \tfrac{1}{2} \times \text{mass} \times \text{velocity}^2$$
$$\text{(J)} \qquad \text{(kg)} \quad \text{([m/s]}^2)$$

> EXAMPLE: A car of mass <u>2450 kg</u> is travelling at <u>38 m/s</u>.
> Calculate its kinetic energy.
>
> ANSWER: Just plug the numbers into the formula, but watch out for the "v²".
> kinetic energy = ½ × mass × velocity² = ½ × 2450 × 38²
> = <u>1 768 900 J</u>   (joules because it's energy)

5) When a force acts on an object it can increase its velocity.

6) The force will have done work on the object.

7) This will increase the kinetic energy of the object.

Increase in K.E. = Work Done. *Just About...*

1) Energy is always conserved.

2) This means you can't make or destroy it — it just gets changed from one kind of energy to another.

3) So, the increase in an object's kinetic energy should be equal to the amount of work that's been done to make it speed up.

4) But some energy gets 'wasted' as heat because of friction and air resistance. So...

> The increase in an object's <u>K.E.</u> is normally <u>a bit less</u> than the amount of <u>work done</u> on it, because some <u>energy is wasted as heat</u>.

5) BUT if there's no friction or air resistance (like in space), OR you're told to ignore it, then the increase in an object's kinetic energy is equal to the amount of work done on it.

After doing all this work you should be bouncing around...

The kinetic energy equation's the hardest one in this module — so make sure you've got it nailed. You'll pick up loads of marks in the exam if you can come up with the right answer and use the correct units — they're joules if you've nodded off. And don't forget that energy is always conserved — otherwise weird things start happening...

Gravitational Potential Energy

It's the last page to learn of this module... and it's got <u>roller coasters</u> on it. Life is good.

G.P.E. is 'Height Energy'

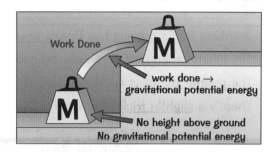

Work Done

work done →
gravitational potential energy

No height above ground
No gravitational potential energy

1) <u>Gravitational potential energy (G.P.E.)</u> is the energy <u>stored in an object</u> when you <u>raise</u> it above the ground.

2) If you <u>lift</u> an object up, its G.P.E. <u>increases</u>.

3) As an object <u>falls</u>, its G.P.E. <u>decreases</u>.

4) The <u>increase</u> in the G.P.E. is <u>equal</u> to the <u>work done</u> by the <u>lifting force</u> to <u>raise</u> its <u>height</u>.

Change in G.P.E. (J) = Weight (N) × Vertical height difference (m)

oh my...

<u>EXAMPLE:</u> A <u>4000 N</u> cow walks onto a hot spring, and is lifted <u>10 m upwards</u>.
Find its change in G.P.E.

<u>ANSWER:</u> Change in G.P.E. = weight × vertical height difference
= 4000 × 10 = <u>40 000 J</u>

Falling Objects Convert G.P.E. into K.E.

1) When something <u>falls</u>, its <u>gravitational potential energy</u> is <u>converted</u> (changed) into <u>kinetic energy (K.E.)</u>.

2) For example, the roller coaster below will <u>lose G.P.E.</u> and <u>gain K.E.</u> as it falls between points <u>A and C</u>.

3) The amount of <u>K.E.</u> it gains will be <u>the same</u> as the amount of <u>G.P.E.</u> it loses
(if we ignore counter forces like <u>friction</u> and <u>air resistance</u>).

K.E. <u>gained</u> = G.P.E. <u>lost</u>

G.P.E.
↓
K.E.

4) So the <u>further</u> it falls, the <u>faster</u> it goes.

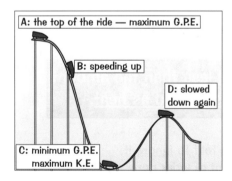

A: the top of the ride — maximum G.P.E.

B: speeding up

D: slowed down again

C: minimum G.P.E.
maximum K.E.

<u>EXAMPLE:</u> The roller coaster car shown weighs <u>5000 N</u>.
The vertical height difference between A and C is <u>20 m</u>.
Ignoring friction and air resistance, how much <u>K.E.</u>
is gained by the carriage in moving from A to C?

<u>ANSWER:</u> K.E. gained = G.P.E. lost
= weight × vertical height difference
= 5000 × 20 = <u>100 000 J</u>

Why did the monkey fall out of the tree? Because it was dead*...

Why did the giraffe fall out of the tree? Because it was dead. Why did the elephant fall out of the tree?
Because he thought it was a game. Tee hee hee. Anyway — back to physics.
Roller coasters are always switching between <u>potential and kinetic energy</u>. In reality, some energy will be lost due
to friction, air resistance and even as sound. But in exams you can usually ignore these.

* Note: no animals were harmed in the making of this revision guide.

Revision Summary for Module P4

Yay — revision summary. I <u>know</u> these are your favourite bits of the book, all those jolly questions. There are lots of equations and picky little details to learn in this module. So, practise these questions till you can do them all standing on one leg with your arms behind your back while being tickled on the nose with a purple ostrich feather. Or something.

1)* Find the speed of a partly chewed mouse which hobbles 3.5 metres in 35 seconds.

$$speed = \frac{distance}{time}$$

2)* A speed camera is set up in a 30 mph (13.3 m/s) zone. It takes two photographs 0.5 s apart. A car travels 6.3 m between the two photographs. Was the car breaking the speed limit?

3) What does the gradient of a distance-time graph tell you?

4) What's the difference between speed and velocity?

5) Sketch a typical speed-time graph and point out all the important points.

6) What is an interaction pair?

7) A man leans on a wall with a force of 50 N. What can you say about the force exerted by the wall?

8) Explain what happens to the drag on a car as it speeds up.

9) Give two everyday examples where forces are balanced. Draw diagrams.

10) What is meant by resultant force?

11)* Find the momentum of a 78 kg sheep moving at 5 m/s.

$$momentum = mass \times velocity$$

12) If an object has zero resultant force on it, can it be moving?

13) Explain how air bags, seat belts and crumple zones reduce the risk of serious injury in a car crash.

14)* A crazy dog dragged a big branch 12 m over the next-door neighbour's front lawn, pulling with a force of 535 N. How much work was done on the branch?

$$work\ done = force \times distance$$

15) Why is the increase in an object's kinetic energy normally a bit less than the amount of work done on it?

16)* Calculate the increase in gravitational potential energy (G.P.E.) when a box of weight 120 N is raised vertically through 4.5 m.

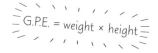
$$G.P.E. = weight \times height$$

17)* A stationary car at the top of a roller coaster has 150 kJ of gravitational potential energy. Ignoring friction and air resistance, how much kinetic energy must it have at the bottom (when G.P.E. = 0)?

Static Electricity

Static electricity's all about <u>charges</u> which are <u>not free to move</u>. This causes them to build up in one place, and lead to <u>sparks</u> or <u>shocks</u> when they finally do move — <u>crackling</u> when you take a jumper off, say.

Build-up of Static is Caused by Rubbing

1) When two objects are <u>rubbed</u> together, <u>electrons</u> are <u>scraped off one</u> and <u>dumped</u> on the other.

2) This leaves a <u>positive</u> (+) static charge on one because <u>electrons</u> (–) have been <u>lost</u>.

3) It leaves a <u>negative</u> (–) static charge on the other one because <u>electrons</u> (–) have been <u>gained</u>.

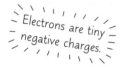

Like Charges Repel, Opposite Charges Attract

1) Two things with <u>opposite</u> electric charges are <u>attracted</u> to each other.

2) Two things with the <u>same</u> electric charge will <u>repel</u> each other (push each other away).

3) When you <u>rub</u> two objects together lots of <u>electrons</u> get dumped <u>together</u> on one of them.

4) The electrons all have the same, <u>negative charge</u>.

5) They <u>try</u> to <u>repel</u> each other, but <u>can't move</u> apart.

6) The patch of charge that results is called <u>static electricity</u> because it can't move.

7) Check out this example of static electricity...

Taking off a Jumper

1) When you drag a <u>jumper</u> over your <u>head</u>, electrons can get <u>pulled off</u>.

2) This leaves a <u>static charge</u> on you and an <u>opposite charge</u> on the jumper.

3) The jumper will start to <u>stick to you</u> as the <u>charges attract</u>.

4) You might feel little <u>shocks</u> as the charges rearrange themselves.

Static caravans — where electrons go on holiday...

Static electricity's great fun. You must have tried rubbing a <u>balloon</u> against your <u>jumper</u> and trying to get it to stick to the ceiling. It really works... well, sometimes. And if at first you don't succeed, try, try again...

Electric Current

Static electricity's all well and good, but things get much more interesting when the charge can move. Moving charge is called current. You can use it to power all sorts of toys and gadgets. It's great stuff.

Electric Current is a Flow of Charge Round a Circuit

1) Electric current is a flow of charge.

2) An electrical circuit is a loop of metal conductors (components and wires).

3) These conductors are full of charges (electrons) that are free to move.

4) So electric current flows in metallic conductors because these free electrons can move around.

5) Current can't flow in an insulator (like plastic) because there are only a few charges free to move.

Batteries Push Charge Round a Circuit

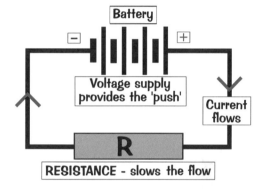

1) The circuit shown here is complete.

2) This means the loop between one side of the battery and the other is continuous.

3) The battery pushes the free charges through the wires.

4) The charge flows all the way round the circuit and back to the battery.

5) It's not used up (it doesn't disappear or anything).

6) Components such as resistors, lamps and motors resist (slow down) the flow of charge.

Current Depends on Voltage and Resistance

1) Current (I) is the flow of charge around a circuit. It's measured in amperes (amps), A.

2) Voltage (V) is the driving force that pushes the current round. Its units are volts, V.

3) Resistance (R) is caused by things in the circuit that slow down the flow of charge. Its units are ohms, Ω.

> The bigger the voltage — the bigger the current.
> The bigger the resistance — the smaller the current.

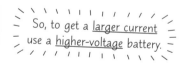
So, to get a larger current use a higher-voltage battery.

Pah, all these jokes are old — can't you find any current ones?

All you've got to remember for this page is that current is the flow of charge, voltage pushes the flow around and resistance tries to stop it. Simple really. Oh yeah, and that electric current can only flow if the electric charges (electrons) are free to move and the circuit is complete. Turn over for another electrifying page...

Power

Mwahahahahaha... Now I've got your attention we're going to learn all about <u>power</u>. That's <u>electrical power</u>, not the world domination, stroking white cats in spinny chairs, evil type power. Pity though.

Power is the Rate of Energy Transfer

1) <u>Power supplies</u> (cells, batteries, etc.) all <u>transfer energy</u> to the <u>charge</u> in a circuit.

2) The charge then transfers energy to the <u>components</u> (and sometimes their <u>surroundings</u>).

3) <u>Work</u> is <u>done</u> because <u>energy is transferred</u> (p. 72).

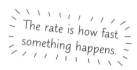
The rate is how fast something happens.

> **POWER** is the **RATE** at which an electrical power supply **TRANSFERS ENERGY** to an appliance.

4) Power is usually measured in <u>watts</u>, **W**, or <u>kilowatts</u>, **kW**.

1 kW = 1000 W

Power of Appliances

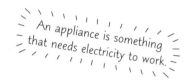
An appliance is something that needs electricity to work.

1) The formula for <u>electrical power</u> is:

> **POWER = VOLTAGE × CURRENT**
> **(W)   (V)   (A)**

2) To find the <u>power</u> of an appliance, just plug in the numbers you're given:

> <u>EXAMPLE:</u> A Mexican dancing robot is rated at <u>9 V</u> and allows a current of <u>11 A</u> to flow.
> Find the power of the dancing robot.
>
> <u>ANSWER:</u> power = voltage × current
> power = 9 V × 11 A = 99 W.

I've got the Power — Dododo do do do...

As revision goes, this topic isn't too bad. <u>Power</u> is just <u>how fast</u> energy can be transferred. Like when the Hulk unleashes his superhuman strength and quickly squashes any bad guy who dares to mess with him. The Hulk unleashed his awesome energy very quickly, therefore the Hulk is very powerful. Simples.

Electric Circuits

We use <u>symbols</u> when we're drawing <u>circuit diagrams</u> as it makes it <u>simpler</u> (even if it doesn't look it at first)...

Circuit Symbols You Should Know:

You'll come across these <u>symbols</u> over the next few pages.
If you <u>learn</u> what they mean it'll make a whole lot <u>more sense</u> later on...

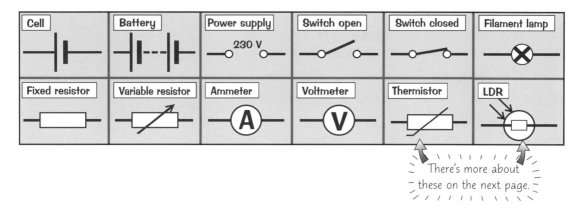

There's more about these on the next page.

A Voltmeter Measures the Potential Difference Between Two Points

1) <u>Potential difference</u> is the proper name for <u>voltage</u>.

2) It tells us how much <u>energy</u> is <u>transferred</u> to or from each <u>charge</u> as it moves between <u>two points</u>.

3) When energy is transferred, <u>work is done</u>.

4) So potential difference also tells us the <u>work done</u> on or by a <u>charge</u> as it moves between two points.

5) The <u>battery</u> transfers energy <u>to</u> the charge as it passes to "<u>push</u>" it round the circuit.

6) The <u>voltage</u> of a battery tells us <u>how big</u> a "<u>push</u>" it gives it.

7) A <u>voltmeter</u> is used to measure the <u>potential difference</u> between <u>two points</u>.

8) A voltmeter must be placed in <u>parallel</u> (see page 82) with a component as shown below.

9) This is so it can <u>compare</u> the energy the charge has <u>before</u> and <u>after</u> passing through the component.

10) An <u>ammeter</u> is used to measure the <u>flow of current</u> through a point in a circuit, e.g. through a component.

11) The ammeter must be placed in <u>series</u> (see page 81) with the component as shown below.

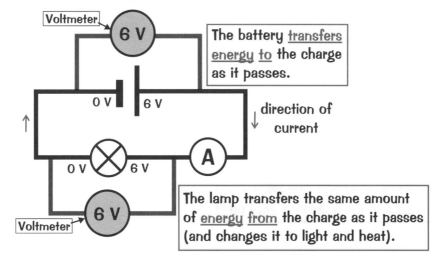

The battery <u>transfers</u> <u>energy</u> <u>to</u> the charge as it passes.

The lamp transfers the same amount of <u>energy</u> <u>from</u> the charge as it passes (and changes it to light and heat).

Why did the lights go out? Because they liked each other... (groan)

An interesting fact — voltage is named after Count Alessandro Volta, an Italian scientist. I heard once that potential difference was named after his cousin — Baron Potentialo Differenché. I'm not so sure if it's true... What is true and very important is that <u>voltage</u> and <u>potential difference</u> are the <u>same</u> thing.

Resistance

Resistors resist the flow of current — simple. Resistors come in all shapes and sizes.
Some have fixed resistance, while others can change their resistance.

The Current Increases When Voltage Increases

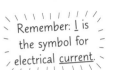
Remember: I is the symbol for electrical current.

1) Voltage-current (V-I) graphs show how the current in a circuit varies as you change the voltage.

2) The current through a component increases as the voltage increases when the resistance stays constant (the same).

3) The current also decreases when the voltage decreases.

4) The wires in an electric circuit have such a small resistance that it's usually ignored.

5) You can use this formula to calculate the resistance of any component:

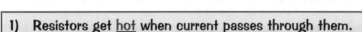

$$\text{Resistance } (\Omega) = \frac{\text{Voltage (V)}}{\text{Current (A)}}$$

1) Resistors get hot when current passes through them.

2) A filament lamp contains a piece of wire with a really high resistance.

3) When current passes through it, its temperature increases so much that it glows — which is the light you see.

Light-Dependent Resistor or "LDR" to You

A light-dependent resistor or LDR is a special type of resistor. Its resistance changes depending on how much light there is:

- In bright light, the resistance falls.
- In darkness, the resistance goes up.

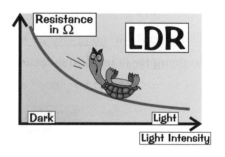

Thermistor (Temperature-Dependent Resistor)

A thermistor is like an LDR — but its resistance depends on temperature.

- In hot conditions, the resistance falls.
- In cool conditions, the resistance goes up.

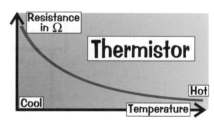

In the end you'll have to learn this — you can't resist...

This page is packed full of useful stuff. You have to be able to describe those voltage-current graphs. That equation's important too — make sure you know how to use it. And now it's on to series circuits... Tally ho...

Series Circuits

You need to be able to tell the difference between series and parallel circuits <u>just by looking at them</u>.

Series Circuits — *Everything in a Line*

In <u>series circuits</u>, components are connected <u>in a line</u>, <u>end to end</u>, between the ends of the battery.

Potential Difference is Shared:

1) In series circuits, the <u>total</u> <u>potential difference</u> (P.D.) of the <u>battery</u> is <u>shared</u> between the <u>components</u>.

2) So the <u>P.D.s</u> of each component <u>add up</u> to the P.D. across the <u>battery</u>:

$$V = V_1 + V_2$$

3) The P.D. is <u>biggest</u> across the component with the <u>biggest resistance</u>.

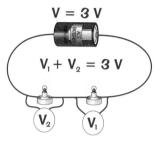

Current is the Same Everywhere:

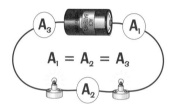

In series circuits the <u>same current</u> flows through <u>each component</u>:

$$A_1 = A_2 = A_3$$

Resistance Adds Up:

1) In series circuits, the <u>total resistance</u> is just the <u>sum</u> of the individual resistances:

$$R = R_1 + R_2$$

2) The resistance of <u>two</u> resistors in <u>series</u> is <u>bigger</u> than the resistance of just one on its own.

3) This is because the <u>battery</u> has to <u>push charge</u> through <u>both</u> of them.

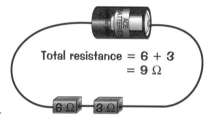

Total resistance = 6 + 3
= 9 Ω

Battery Voltages Add Up:

1) If you connect <u>several batteries in series</u>, <u>all the same way</u> (+ to −) you get a <u>bigger total voltage</u>.

2) This is because the charge gets a 'push' from <u>each one</u> in turn.

3) So <u>two 1.5 V</u> batteries <u>in series</u> would supply <u>3 V in total</u>.

4) The <u>current</u> in the circuit <u>increases</u> because the <u>voltage increases</u>.

Series circuits — they're no laughing matter...

If you connect some <u>lamps</u> in <u>series</u> and one of them <u>breaks</u> then <u>all</u> of them stop working. This is <u>unhelpful</u>.

Parallel Circuits

Parallel circuits are much more <u>sensible</u> than series circuits so they're much more <u>common</u> in <u>real life</u>.

Parallel Circuits — Everything Connected Separately

In <u>parallel circuits</u>, each component is <u>separately</u> connected to the ends of the battery.

Total Current is Shared Between Branches:

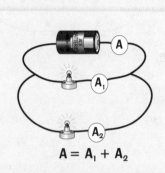

$A = A_1 + A_2$

1) In parallel circuits, the <u>current</u> flowing from the battery is <u>shared</u> between the branches.

2) So the <u>total current</u> from (and back to) the battery is the <u>total</u> of the currents through <u>each component</u>:

$$A = A_1 + A_2$$

3) The component with the <u>least</u> resistance has the <u>largest</u> current.

Total Resistance is Less than the Smallest One:

1) The <u>total resistance</u> of a parallel circuit is always <u>less</u> than the resistance of the component with the <u>smallest</u> resistance.

2) This is because the charge has <u>more than one</u> path to take.

3) So only <u>some</u> of the charge will flow along each path.

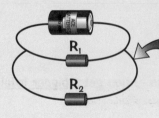

R_1

R_2

The total resistance is less than the resistance of R_1 and R_2.

A current shared — is a current halved...*

Parallel circuits might look a bit scarier than series ones, but they're much more useful. Remember that the <u>current</u> is <u>shared</u> between branches and the <u>total resistance</u> is <u>lower</u> than that of the least resistant branch. Phew — that's a lot to take in but it'll all be worth it in the end. Honest.

* Conditions may apply. CGP takes no responsibility for the accuracy of this proverb.

Mains Electricity

It's difficult to imagine a world <u>without electricity</u>. It would be hard to bake cakes at night, for a start.

Mains Supply is a.c., Battery Supply is d.c.

This is the stuff you get from plug sockets at home.

1) The UK <u>mains domestic electricity supply</u> is <u>230 volts</u>.

2) It's produced by <u>generators</u> using a process called <u>electromagnetic induction</u> (see below).

3) Mains electricity is an <u>a.c. supply</u> (alternating current) — the current is always <u>changing direction</u>.

4) Batteries are a <u>d.c. supply</u> (direct current) — the current always flows in the <u>same direction</u>.

Moving a Magnet into a Coil of Wire Induces a Voltage

1) You can <u>induce</u> (create) a <u>voltage</u> in a conductor by <u>moving a magnet</u> into a <u>coil of wire</u>.

2) This is called <u>electromagnetic induction</u>.

3) If the ends of the wire are <u>connected</u> to make a <u>complete circuit</u> then a <u>current</u> will flow in the wire.

4) The <u>direction</u> of the voltage depends on <u>which way</u> you <u>move the magnet</u>:

If you <u>move</u> the magnet <u>into</u> the coil the voltage is induced in the <u>opposite</u> direction from when you move it <u>out</u> of the coil.	If you <u>switch</u> the magnet's North and South ends — so that the opposite <u>end</u> points into the coil, the voltage is induced in the <u>opposite</u> direction.
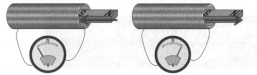	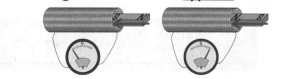

Four Factors Affect the Size of the Induced Voltage

1) In a <u>generator</u>, a <u>magnet</u> or an <u>electromagnet</u> <u>rotates</u> (turns) inside a coil of wire.

2) This induces a <u>voltage</u> across the ends of the coil.

3) If you want a <u>bigger</u> voltage (and current) you could do one or more of these <u>four things</u>:

> 1) <u>Add</u> an <u>IRON CORE</u> inside the coil
> 2) <u>Increase</u> the <u>STRENGTH</u> of the <u>MAGNETIC FIELD</u>
> 3) <u>Increase</u> the <u>SPEED</u> of <u>ROTATION</u>
> 4) <u>Increase</u> the number of <u>TURNS</u> on the <u>COIL</u>

To reduce the voltage, you would reduce one of the factors or take the iron core out.

So THAT's how they make electricity — I always wondered...

Generators are mostly powered by <u>burning things</u> to make <u>steam</u>, that turns a turbine, that turns the magnet. You can get portable generators too, to use in places without mains electricity — like at music festivals.

Transformers and Magnetic Fields

So you've generated your electricity, but it's not at the right <u>voltage</u>. What do you need? A <u>transformer</u>.

Transformers *Change a.c. Voltages*

1) <u>Transformers</u> are used to change the <u>size</u> of an <u>alternating voltage</u>.

2) They are made from <u>two coils of wire</u> wound around an <u>iron core</u>.

3) The <u>alternating current</u> in one coil causes <u>changes</u> in the iron core's <u>magnetic field</u> (see below).

4) This <u>induces</u> a <u>changing voltage</u> in the second coil.

Alternating means it keeps changing direction.

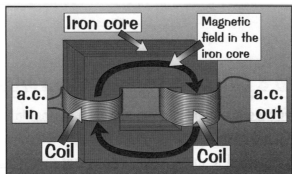

The size of the voltage induced depends on the number of turns on each coil.

Magnets *and* Current-Carrying Wires *Have Magnetic Fields*

A <u>MAGNETIC FIELD</u> is an area where <u>MAGNETIC MATERIALS</u> (like iron and steel) and also <u>WIRES CARRYING CURRENTS</u> feel a <u>FORCE</u> acting on them.

A Current-Carrying Wire *Creates a Magnetic Field*

1) There is a <u>magnetic field</u> around a <u>straight</u>, <u>current-carrying wire</u>.

2) It looks a bit like this:

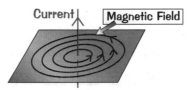

A Rectangular Coil *Reinforces the Magnetic Field*

1) If you <u>bend</u> the current-carrying wire round into a <u>coil</u>, the magnetic field looks like this.

2) The circular magnetic fields around the sides of the loop <u>reinforce</u> (add to) each other at the <u>centre</u> creating a <u>stronger</u> magnetic field.

3) If the coil has <u>lots of turns</u>, the magnetic fields from all the individual loops reinforce each other <u>even more</u>.

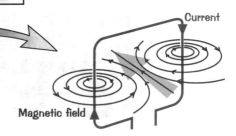

Which transformer do you need to enslave the Universe? Megatron...

Yikes, wires and coils creating forces. Who would have thought it. This stuff is all really important though... You need to make sure you've learnt it properly as there's a lot more on magnetic fields to come. Yippee.

Magnetic Fields

This stuff's a bit tricky to get your head around so <u>concentrate</u>...

A Current in a Magnetic Field Experiences a Force

1) Because of its magnetic field, a <u>current-carrying wire</u> or <u>coil</u> can exert a <u>force</u> on <u>another</u> current-carrying wire or coil, or on a <u>permanent magnet</u>.

2) When a current-carrying wire is put in a <u>different</u> magnetic field, the <u>two</u> magnetic fields <u>affect one another</u>.

3) The result is a <u>force</u> on the <u>wire</u>.

4) To feel the <u>full force</u>, the <u>wire</u> has to be at <u>right-angles</u> (90°) to the <u>lines of force</u> of the <u>magnetic field</u> it's placed in (as shown in the diagram below).

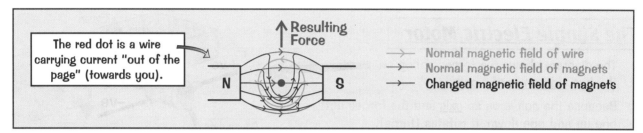

The red dot is a wire carrying current "out of the page" (towards you).

→ Normal magnetic field of wire
→ Normal magnetic field of magnets
→ Changed magnetic field of magnets

5) As shown in the diagram, the <u>force</u> will act at <u>right-angles</u> to <u>both</u> the magnetic field lines <u>and</u> the direction of the current. You can work out which way this is by using Fleming's left-hand rule — see below.

6) If the wire runs <u>parallel</u> to the lines of force of the magnetic field, it feels <u>no force</u>.

Fleming's Left-Hand Rule Tells You Which Way the Force Acts

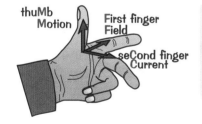

thuMb Motion
First finger Field
seCond finger Current

1) Using your <u>left hand</u>, point your <u>First finger</u> in the direction of the <u>magnetic Field</u>.

2) Point your <u>seCond finger</u> in the direction of the wire's <u>Current</u>.

3) Your <u>thuMb</u> will then point in the direction of the <u>force</u> (Motion). Wow.

(Give it a try with the diagram of the wire and the magnet field above.)

They won't mention Fleming's left-hand rule in the exam but it'll be really useful when you have to work out which way the force is going to act.

Use the force — at right-angles to the magnetic field...

When I'm <u>parallel</u> to my bed I don't feel any force pulling me out of it. Just like wires and magnets... Sort of. This might all seem a bit complicated at first but Fleming's <u>left-hand rule</u> should help a bit. Make sure you can work out which <u>direction</u> the <u>force</u> is going to act in for that diagram above and you'll be fine.

The Motor Effect

The motor effect — that's how electric motors work. Should be easy to remember that.

Magnetic Fields Make Current-Carrying Coils Turn

1) If a rectangular coil of wire carrying a current is placed in a uniform magnetic field, the force will cause it to turn.

2) This is called the motor effect.

3) You can use Fleming's left-hand rule from the previous page to work out which way the coil will turn.

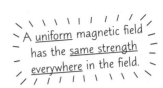
A uniform magnetic field has the same strength everywhere in the field.

The Simple Electric Motor

1) The diagram shows the forces acting on the two side arms of a coil.

2) Because the coil is on an axis and the forces act one up and one down, it rotates (turns).

3) The commutator is used to reverse the direction of the current every half-turn to keep the coil rotating continuously in the same direction.

4) Without a commutator, the direction of the force would reverse every half-turn and the coil would change direction instead of fully rotating.

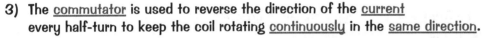

Anything That Uses Rotation can be Powered by an Electric Motor

1) Lots of devices use rotation.

2) They all work by using an electric motor in a similar way.

3) If you link the coil in a motor to an axle, the axle spins round.

4) In the diagram there's a fan attached to the axle, but you can stick almost anything on a motor axle and make it spin round.

5) For example:

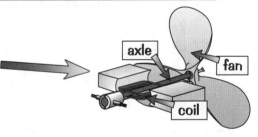

- In a DVD player, the axle's attached to the bit the DVD sits on to make it spin.

- Electric cars and trains have their wheels attached to axles.

- Electric motors spin the platters (the bits where information is stored) of a computer hard disc drive.

- Domestic appliances, such as washing machines, fridges and vacuum cleaners, all use electric motors.

Hello Motor...

Loudspeakers use the motor effect. Electrical signals make a coil move over the poles of a magnet. These movements make the cardboard cone vibrate and this creates sounds. So next time your P.E. teacher is yelling at you through one you can thank the good old motor effect.

Revision Summary for Module P5

There's some pretty heavy physics in this module. But just take it one page at a time and it's not so bad. When you think you know it all, try these questions and see how you're getting on. If there are any you can't do, look back at the right page, learn it, then come back here and try again.

1) What causes the build-up of static electricity?

2) Describe the forces between objects with: a) like charges,   b) opposite charges.

3) Explain how static electricity can make clothes crackle when you take them off.

4) Explain why electric current can flow in metals.

5) Explain what current, voltage and resistance are in an electric circuit.

6) What happens to the amount of current in a circuit if the voltage of the battery is increased?

7) What does the power of an appliance measure?

8)* A remote controlled helicopter has a voltage of 230 V and a current of 5 A.
    What is its power?

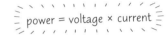

power = voltage × current

9) What is another name for voltage?

10) Sketch a typical voltage-current graph for a constant resistance.

11)* Calculate the resistance of a wire if the voltage across it is 12 V
     and the current through it is 2.5 A.

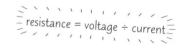

resistance = voltage ÷ current

12) Describe how the resistance of an LDR varies with light intensity.

13) What happens to the voltage when several batteries are added to a series circuit?

14) Two circuits each contain a 2 Ω and a 4 Ω resistor — in one circuit
    they're in series, in the other they're in parallel. Which circuit will
    have the <u>higher</u> total resistance? Why?

15) What voltage is UK mains electricity supplied at?

16) Explain what electromagnetic induction is.

17) Explain how a generator works.

18) What are the four factors that affect the size of the induced voltage produced by a generator?

19) What are transformers used for?

20) A current-carrying wire runs parallel to the lines of force of a magnetic field. Does the wire feel a force?

21) Where does a wire have to be placed to feel the full force of a magnetic field?

22) What part of an electric motor reverses the direction of the current?

23) Briefly describe three uses of electric motors.

The Nucleus

Radioactivity — nothing to do with how much you use your radio. It's much more interesting than that.

Atoms Have a Nucleus Surrounded by Electrons

1) The nucleus of an atom contains protons and neutrons.

2) It's tiny, but contains most of the mass.

3) Electrons are really really small.

4) They whizz around the outside of the atom, and take up a lot of space.

5) This gives the atom its size even though an atom is mostly empty space.

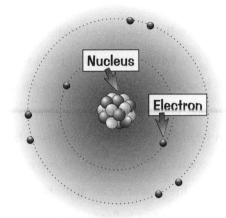

Rutherford's Experiment Showed that Atoms Have a Positive Nucleus

1) In 1909, three scientists named Rutherford, Geiger and Marsden fired alpha particles at thin gold foil.

2) Most of the alpha particles just went straight through the foil.

3) But a few of the alpha particles came straight back at them.

4) Alpha particles are small and positively charged, so this meant that:

   a) most of the atom must be empty space — as most of the alpha particles went straight through the foil.

   b) most of the mass of an atom is concentrated at the centre in a tiny nucleus.

   c) the nucleus must have a positive charge because the positive alpha particles were repelled by the gold nucleus and scattered.

Two positive charges will repel each other (see page 76).

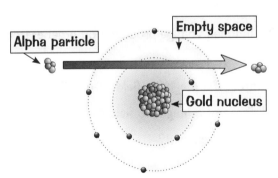

Most alpha particles pass through the empty space in a gold atom.

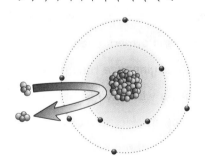

Some alpha particles are repelled by the positively charged nucleus.

Rutherford, Geiger and Marsden walk into a bar...

...Ouch. Ouch. Ouch. Anyway, if atoms are mostly empty space and everything is made of atoms then everything is mostly empty space. Weird. Remember, things which have the same charge as each other repel each other. We know that alpha particles are positive and the nucleus repels them, so it must be positive too.

Radioactivity and Half-Life

The three types of ionising radiation (<u>alpha</u>, <u>beta</u> and <u>gamma</u>) are all emitted by radioactive materials.

Radioactive Elements Give Out Ionising Radiation

1) Ionising radiation is a type of radiation that can <u>break</u> an atom or molecule into <u>bits</u> called <u>ions</u>.

2) The <u>three types</u> of ionising radiation are called <u>alpha</u>, <u>beta</u> and <u>gamma</u>.

3) Some <u>elements</u> emit (give out) <u>ionising radiation</u> all the time. These elements are <u>radioactive</u>.

4) You <u>can't change</u> when or how radioactive elements give out ionising radiation.

5) They are not affected by <u>physical</u> conditions (like <u>temperature</u>) or <u>chemical processes</u> (like <u>bonding</u>).

Remember What Stops the Three Types of Ionising Radiation

1) <u>Alpha</u> particles <u>don't penetrate</u> far into materials — they're stopped easily by paper.

2) <u>Beta</u> particles <u>penetrate further</u> — they're stopped by aluminium foil.

3) <u>Gamma</u> rays can <u>penetrate a long way</u> — they're only stopped by thick lead.

Penetration means how easily something passes through something else.

Similar things will also block them. Skin will stop alpha, a thin sheet of any metal will stop beta, and very thick concrete will stop gamma.

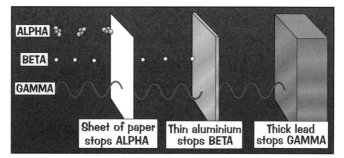

ALPHA   BETA   GAMMA

Sheet of paper stops ALPHA   Thin aluminium stops BETA   Thick lead stops GAMMA

The Activity of a Sample Decreases Over Time

1) <u>Ionising radiation</u> is given out when a nucleus <u>decays</u>. How often this happens is called the <u>activity</u>.

2) Each time a nucleus decays, there's <u>one less</u> left to give out radiation <u>later</u>.

3) So, over time, the <u>activity</u> of a sample of a radioactive element <u>decreases</u>.

4) <u>How quickly</u> the activity <u>decreases</u> varies a lot.

5) For <u>some</u> radioactive elements it takes <u>just a few seconds</u> to drop to almost nothing.
   For others it can take <u>millions of years</u>.

6) We use <u>half-life</u> to measure <u>how quickly the activity decreases</u>:

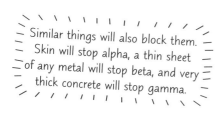

HALF-LIFE is the <u>TIME TAKEN</u> for the <u>ACTIVITY</u> of a sample to <u>HALVE</u>.

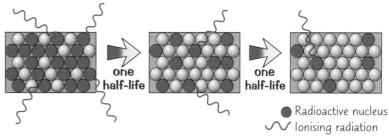

one half-life   one half-life

● Radioactive nucleus
〰 Ionising radiation

6) A <u>short half-life</u> means the <u>activity falls quickly</u>.

7) A <u>long half-life</u> means the activity <u>falls slowly</u>.

Half-life of a box of chocolates — about five minutes...

To measure half-life, you time how <u>long it takes</u> for the activity of a radioactive element to <u>halve</u>. Sweet.

Fusion, Fission and Nuclear Power

Ooooh... This page pretty cool. It's got loads of <u>proper physics</u> to keep you entertained.

Nuclei **Can** Fuse Together

Nuclei just means more than one nucleus.

1) <u>Two nuclei</u> can <u>combine</u> (<u>fuse</u>) to create a <u>larger nucleus</u>.

2) This process is called <u>nuclear fusion</u>.

3) Nuclei <u>release energy</u> when they fuse.

4) For example, <u>hydrogen</u> nuclei can fuse together to make <u>helium</u> nuclei.

Hydrogen

Hydrogen

fusion

Energy

Helium

Nuclear Fuels **Release Energy** When the **Nucleus Changes**

1) A <u>nuclear fuel</u> releases <u>large amounts of energy</u> when its nuclei <u>split apart</u>.

2) This process is called <u>nuclear fission</u>.

3) <u>Nuclear</u> reactions, like fission and fusion, release <u>a lot more energy</u> than <u>chemical</u> reactions (like burning).

4) For example, splitting a <u>gram</u> of <u>uranium</u> (a <u>nuclear</u> fuel) releases over <u>10 000 times</u> more energy than burning a <u>gram</u> of <u>oil</u> (a <u>chemical</u> fuel).

big nucleus

fission

smaller nuclei

energy

The **Waste** from Nuclear **Power Stations** <u>is Hard to Deal With</u>

1) Nuclear <u>fuels</u> are used in <u>nuclear power stations</u>.

2) Nuclear power stations produce <u>radioactive waste</u>.

3) <u>Low level</u> (<u>slightly</u> radioactive) waste can be disposed of by <u>burying</u> it in secure landfill sites.

4) <u>Intermediate level</u> (<u>quite</u> radioactive) waste is often sealed into <u>concrete blocks</u> then put in <u>steel containers</u> for storage.

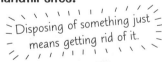

Disposing of something just means getting rid of it.

5) <u>High level</u> (<u>very</u> radioactive) waste is <u>so radioactive</u> that it makes a lot of <u>heat</u>.

6) This waste is sealed up in <u>glass</u> and <u>steel</u>, then <u>cooled</u> in ponds of <u>water</u> for about <u>50 years</u>.

7) It can then be moved to more <u>long-term</u> storage (such as being buried <u>deep underground</u>).

Fuse this page into your brain — don't let it go to waste...

There's enough <u>nuclear fuel</u> in the world to provide us with <u>energy</u> for years, but it's hard to deal with the <u>radioactive waste</u>. You need to know all about the three 'levels' of waste and how they're <u>disposed</u> of.

Danger from Ionising Radiation

Radioactive materials can be really <u>dangerous</u>. Eeeeek.

Ionising Radiation can Damage Living Cells

1) All types of <u>ionising radiation</u> can cause <u>serious damage</u> to cells in the body.

2) A large amount of radiation will <u>kill cells</u>, causing <u>radiation sickness</u>.

3) Smaller amounts <u>damage cells</u> without killing them, which can cause <u>cancer</u>.

4) Radioactive materials can harm people through either:

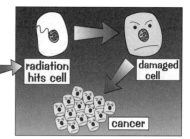

> a) <u>IRRADIATION</u> — being exposed to radiation <u>without touching</u> any radioactive material. The damage to your body <u>stops</u> as soon as you leave the radioactive area.
>
> b) <u>CONTAMINATION</u> — <u>picking up</u> some radioactive material, by <u>breathing it in</u>, <u>drinking</u> contaminated water or getting it on your <u>skin</u>. You take the radioactive material with you, so you'll <u>still</u> be exposed to radiation once you've <u>left</u> the radioactive area.

Being exposed to radiation means it can get to you.

Sieverts Show Possible Harm from Ionising Radiation

1) Radiation <u>dose</u> is a measure of the <u>possible harm</u> done to your body by <u>radiation</u>.

2) It is measured in <u>sieverts</u> (<u>Sv</u>) or more usually <u>millisieverts</u> (<u>mSv</u>).

3) The dose depends on the <u>type</u> and <u>amount of radiation</u> you've been exposed to.

4) The following data shows some radiation doses and their <u>effects</u> on the body:

You might have to interpret data on radiation dose. There's more on interpreting data on pages 95-97.

2 mSv/year	Average background radiation dose (see page 92) received by everyone.
20 mSv/year	Current dose limit for people exposed to ionising radiation because of their work.
100 mSv/year	Lowest dose which definitely increases the risk of getting cancer.
1000 mSv/dose	Causes radiation sickness.
5000 mSv/dose	Would kill about half the people who received it within a month.
10 000 mSv/dose	Fatal within a few weeks.

Data from the World Nuclear Association

5) The <u>types</u> of people who are exposed to radiation more often include:

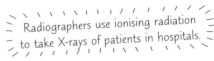

- workers in <u>nuclear power stations</u>
- some <u>medical</u> staff (such as <u>radiographers</u>)

Radiographers use ionising radiation to take X-rays of patients in hospitals.

6) These types of people have their radiation doses carefully <u>monitored</u>.

Revision sickness — never mind, it'll all be worth it...

<u>Everyone</u> is exposed to <u>some</u> radiation (see next page). But don't worry, the average dose is <u>10 times</u> less than the limit for people who <u>work</u> with radiation, and even that seems to be <u>pretty safe</u> (as far as we know).

Using Ionising Radiation

Sometimes ionising radiation can actually be quite <u>useful</u>.

Ionising Radiation Can be Very Useful

1) <u>Tracers</u> are <u>radioactive molecules</u> that can be <u>injected</u> into people.

2) They can be used to <u>detect cancer</u> or whether an organ is <u>working properly</u>.

3) High doses of <u>gamma rays</u> are used to <u>kill cancer cells</u>.

4) <u>Gamma rays</u> are also used to <u>sterilise medical instruments</u> by <u>killing</u> all the microbes.

5) <u>Food</u> can be sterilised in the same way as medical instruments — again <u>killing</u> all the microbes.

6) The food is <u>not</u> radioactive afterwards, so it's <u>safe</u> to eat.

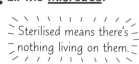

Microbes are tiny living things, like bacteria.

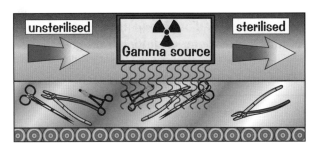

Sterilised means there's nothing living on them.

Background Radiation is Everywhere All the Time

1) There's <u>ionising radiation</u> all around us that is constantly <u>irradiating</u> and <u>contaminating</u> us.

2) This is called <u>background radiation</u>.

3) Background radiation comes from:

> a) <u>NATURAL RADIOACTIVE ELEMENTS</u> in the <u>air</u>, in <u>soil</u>, in <u>living things</u> and in the <u>rocks</u> under our feet.
>
> b) <u>SPACE</u> (cosmic rays), mostly from the <u>Sun</u>.
>
> c) <u>HUMAN ACTIVITY</u>, such as <u>nuclear explosions</u> or <u>waste from nuclear power stations</u>.

Background Radiation is at a Safe Level

1) The <u>activity</u> of a sample of a radioactive element gets <u>lower</u> over time (see page 89).

2) It is said to be <u>safe</u> when its activity is about the <u>same level</u> as the <u>background radiation</u>.

3) The <u>half-life</u> of the element lets us work out <u>how long</u> it will take for a sample to become safe.

Gamma radiation — just what the doctor ordered...

Background radiation was discovered <u>accidentally</u>. Scientists couldn't understand why their detector showed radioactivity when there was <u>no material</u> being tested. They were picking up background radiation.

Revision Summary for Module P6

Phew... what a relief — you made it to the end of yet another section. But don't run off to put the kettle on just yet. Make sure that you really know your stuff with these revision questions.

1) Name the two types of particle found in the nucleus of an atom.

2) Name the particle that whizzes around the outside of an atom.

3) Why do most alpha particles pass through gold foil?

4) Alpha particles are positively charged. What type of charge does a gold nucleus have?

5) Name three types of ionising radiation.

6) Can you change how a radioactive element gives out radiation?

7) Which type of ionising radiation penetrates the furthest?

8) What does half-life mean?

9) Briefly describe what happens when two atoms of hydrogen fuse together.

10) How is low level radioactive waste disposed of?

11) What happens to a cell that receives a high dose of ionising radiation?

12) What units are doses of radiation measured in?

13) Give two types of people who are exposed to radiation more often.

14) Give three uses of ionising radiation.

15) Name a source of background radiation.

Planning

Your controlled assessment is a <u>practical investigation</u>. To start with, you'll be given some material to get your head around. Here's what you'll need to do:

1) Come up with a <u>hypothesis</u> to test based on the information you've been given.

2) <u>Plan</u> an experiment to test your hypothesis. You'll need to think about things like:
   * What you're going to <u>measure</u> and <u>how</u> you're going to do it (your <u>method</u>).
   * What <u>equipment</u> you're going to use (and <u>why</u> that equipment is <u>right for the job</u>).
   * How you're going to make sure your results are <u>accurate</u> and <u>reliable</u>.

3) Write a <u>risk assessment</u> for the experiment.

4) <u>Explain</u> all the choices you made in your <u>plan</u>.

Here are a few <u>tips</u> to help you with the planning stage:

Think Carefully About the <u>Method</u> and <u>Equipment</u> You'll Use

1) Your method needs to give you <u>reliable results</u>.

2) Reliable results are results that are <u>always the same</u> each time you do an experiment.

3) You can make your results <u>more reliable</u> if you make your method a <u>fair test</u>.

4) To make it a fair test you usually <u>change one thing</u> (a variable) and <u>measure</u> how it affects <u>another thing</u> (another variable).

> **EXAMPLE:** you might change only the supply voltage of a circuit and measure how it affects the current.

5) <u>Everything else</u> that could affect the results needs to <u>stay the same</u>.
   Then you know that the thing you're <u>changing</u> is the <u>only</u> thing that's affecting the results.

> **EXAMPLE** continued: you need to keep the resistance the same. If you don't, you won't know if any change in the current is caused by the change in voltage, or the change in resistance.

6) <u>Repeating</u> the readings and working out the <u>mean</u> (average) will also make your results more reliable.

7) Your results need to be <u>accurate</u> too.
   This means that they're <u>really close</u> to the <u>true answer</u>.

8) To get <u>accurate results</u>, you need to choose <u>the right equipment</u>. For example, the <u>measuring equipment</u> you use has to <u>accurately measure</u> the chemicals you're using. If you need to measure <u>11 ml</u> of a liquid, use a measuring cylinder that can measure to <u>1 ml</u>, not <u>5 or 10 ml</u>.

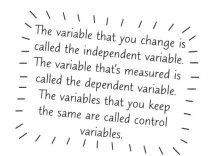

The variable that you change is called the independent variable. The variable that's measured is called the dependent variable. The variables that you keep the same are called control variables.

Experiments Must be <u>Safe</u>

1) Part of planning an investigation is making sure that it'll be <u>safe</u>.

2) You should always make sure that you think of all the <u>hazards</u> (dangers) that you might come across.

3) You should also come up with ways of <u>reducing the risks</u> from the hazards you've spotted.

4) Do this by carrying out a <u>risk assessment</u>. E.g. if you're using a <u>Bunsen burner</u>, there would be a <u>fire risk</u>. To reduce the risk, you'd have to do things like stand the Bunsen on a heat proof mat.

Processing the Data

Once you've planned your experiment you'll carry it out to <u>collect your own data</u> (called <u>primary data</u>). You'll then be <u>given</u> some <u>secondary data</u> (that's data <u>collected by someone else</u>). You'll also need to <u>find more secondary data</u> yourself, e.g. from textbooks or websites. You'll need to <u>process</u> and <u>analyse</u> all the data you have. This might involve a few different things:

1) <u>Laying-out</u> and <u>organising</u> your data using <u>tables</u>.

2) Doing mathematical <u>calculations</u> to <u>process</u> your data.

3) Drawing <u>graphs</u> or <u>diagrams</u> to <u>display</u> your data.

4) Looking for <u>patterns</u> in your data.

Data Needs to be Organised

1) Data that's been collected needs to be <u>organised</u> so it can be processed.

2) <u>Tables</u> are dead useful for organising data.

3) Tables are also good for spotting any <u>outliers</u> (see page 3).

4) When drawing tables, make sure that <u>each column</u> has a <u>heading</u> and that you've included the <u>units</u>.

Data Can be Processed Using a Bit of Maths

1) <u>Raw data</u> just isn't that useful. You usually have to <u>process</u> it in some way.

2) One of the simplest calculations you can do is the <u>mean</u> (average):

- To calculate the <u>mean</u> **ADD TOGETHER** all the data values and **DIVIDE** by the total number of values.
- You usually do this to get a single value from several <u>repeats</u> of your experiment.

Different Types of Data Should be Presented in Different Ways

1) You'll need to <u>present</u> your data so that it's easier to see any <u>patterns</u>.

2) Different types of investigations give you <u>different types</u> of data. You'll always have to <u>choose</u> what the best way to present your data is.

Bar Charts

1) If the independent variable comes in <u>clear categories</u> (e.g. blood types, metals) you should use a <u>bar chart</u> to display the data.

2) There are some <u>golden rules</u> you need to follow for <u>drawing</u> bar charts:

Don't forget — the independent variable is the variable that you change.

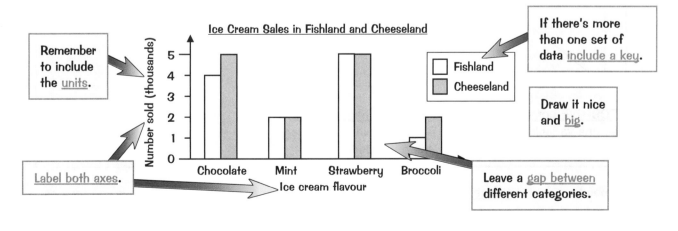

Remember to include the <u>units</u>.

If there's more than one set of data <u>include a key</u>.

Draw it nice and <u>big</u>.

<u>Label both axes.</u>

Leave a <u>gap between</u> different categories.

Ice Cream Sales in Fishland and Cheeseland

Number sold (thousands) — Ice cream flavour: Chocolate, Mint, Strawberry, Broccoli

Fishland / Cheeseland

Processing the Data

Hold up, you haven't finished with <u>data processing</u> yet, and there's still the <u>analysis</u> to think about. Sheesh.

Line Graphs

If the independent variable can have <u>any value</u> within a <u>range</u>, (e.g. length, volume, temperature) you should use a <u>line graph</u> to display the data.

Remember to include the <u>units</u>.

The <u>dependent</u> variable (the thing you measure) goes on the <u>y-axis</u> (the <u>vertical</u> one).

The <u>independent</u> variable (the thing you change) goes on the <u>x-axis</u> (the <u>horizontal</u> one).

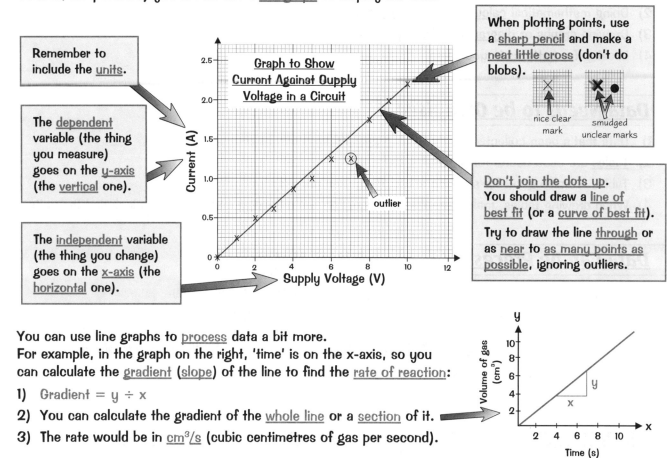

When plotting points, use a <u>sharp pencil</u> and make a <u>neat little cross</u> (don't do blobs).

nice clear mark

smudged unclear marks

<u>Don't join the dots up.</u> You should draw a <u>line of best fit</u> (or a <u>curve of best fit</u>).

Try to draw the line <u>through</u> or as <u>near</u> to <u>as many points as possible</u>, ignoring outliers.

Graph to Show Current Against Supply Voltage in a Circuit

outlier

You can use line graphs to <u>process</u> data a bit more.
For example, in the graph on the right, 'time' is on the x-axis, so you can calculate the <u>gradient</u> (<u>slope</u>) of the line to find the <u>rate of reaction</u>:

1) Gradient = y ÷ x
2) You can calculate the gradient of the <u>whole line</u> or a <u>section</u> of it.
3) The rate would be in <u>cm³/s</u> (cubic centimetres of gas per second).

Line Graphs Can Show Relationships in Data

Before you can make any conclusions, you need to look for <u>relationships</u> between variables.

1) <u>Line graphs</u> are great for showing relationships between two variables.

2) Here are the <u>three</u> different types of <u>correlation</u> (relationship) shown on line graphs:

There's more on correlation on page 4.

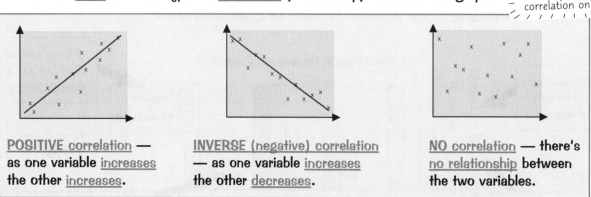

<u>POSITIVE</u> correlation — as one variable <u>increases</u> the other <u>increases</u>.

<u>INVERSE</u> (negative) correlation — as one variable <u>increases</u> the other <u>decreases</u>.

<u>NO</u> correlation — there's <u>no relationship</u> between the two variables.

3) Remember, don't <u>confuse correlation</u> with <u>cause</u> — there might be <u>other factors</u> involved (see page 4).

Conclusion and Evaluation

At the end of your practical investigation, the <u>conclusion</u> and <u>evaluation</u> will be waiting.
Don't worry, they won't bite. Here's what you'll need to do:

1) Draw a <u>conclusion</u> from your primary data and draw a conclusion from your secondary data.
   Then <u>compare</u> the two conclusions and say how well the secondary data supports the primary data.

2) Look back at your <u>hypothesis</u> and say how well the conclusions <u>support it</u>
   (whether they say the same thing or not).

3) Look critically at your <u>method</u> and your <u>results</u> and write an <u>evaluation</u> of your investigation.

I know, I know, it's all very exciting. I bet you can't wait to get on with it...

A Conclusion is a Summary of What You've Learnt

1) To draw a conclusion, just <u>look at your data</u> and <u>say what pattern you see</u>.

EXAMPLE: The table on the right shows the rate of a reaction in the presence of two different chemicals.

Chemical	Rate of reaction (cm³/s)
A	13.5
B	19.5
No chemical	5.5

CONCLUSION:
Chemical <u>B</u> makes <u>this reaction</u> go faster than chemical A.

2) You should use the data that's been <u>collected</u> to <u>back up</u> your conclusion.

EXAMPLE continued... The rate of this reaction was 6 cm³/s faster using chemical B compared with chemical A.

3) You should also use your own <u>scientific knowledge</u> (the stuff you've learnt in class)
   to <u>explain</u> how well your conclusion supports the original <u>hypothesis</u>.

4) If the conclusion <u>agrees</u> with the hypothesis, then it <u>increases confidence</u> in the hypothesis
   (makes us more sure that it's right).

5) If the conclusion <u>doesn't agree</u> with the hypothesis, then it <u>decreases confidence</u> in the hypothesis
   (makes us less sure that it's right).

Evaluation — Weigh Up How Well Things Went

1) An evaluation involves being <u>honest</u> and pointing out the <u>problems</u> with your investigation.

   • You should comment on the <u>method</u> — was the <u>equipment suitable</u>?
     Was it a <u>fair test</u>?

   • Comment on the <u>quality</u> of the <u>results</u> — was there <u>enough evidence</u>
     to reach a valid <u>conclusion</u>?

   • Were the results <u>reliable</u>, <u>accurate</u> and <u>precise</u>?

   • Were there any <u>outliers</u> in the results — if there were <u>none</u> then <u>say so</u>.

   • If there were any outliers, try to <u>explain</u> them — were they caused by
     <u>errors</u> in measurement?

I'd value this E somewhere in the region of 250-300k

2) After you've done the evaluation, explain how you would <u>collect more data</u>
   to <u>increase confidence</u> in the hypothesis.

3) Even if there were <u>no problems</u> with your investigation, your <u>conclusion</u> might still <u>not match</u>
   the <u>hypothesis</u>. If this happens, you should suggest how to <u>change</u> the hypothesis so that it
   <u>matches</u> your conclusion.

4) You could then suggest ways to test the new hypothesis with <u>further experiments</u>.

Index

Index

Index

Answers

Revision Summary for Module B5 (page 19)

	Mitosis	Meiosis
Its purpose is to provide new cells for growth and repair.	✓	✗
Its purpose is to create gametes (sex cells).	✗	✓
The cells produced are genetically identical.	✓	✗
The cells produced contain half the number of chromosomes that were in the parent cell.	✗	✓

Revision Summary for Module C4 (page 38)

3) 4

10) 8

Calculating Masses (page 47)

1) Cu — 63.5
   K — 39
   Kr — 84
   Cl — 35.5

2) NaOH — 23 + 16 + 1 = 40
   HNO_3 — 1 + 14 + (16 × 3) = 63
   KCl — 39 + 35.5 = 74.5
   $CaCO_3$ — 40 + 12 + (16 × 3) = 100

Revision Summary for Module C5 (page 50)

4) C_2H_6

15) a) 40
    b) 108
    c) 44
    d) 84
    e) 78
    f) 106

16) a) 24 + 16 = 40 g
    b) 56 × 2 = 112 g

Calculating Masses in Reactions (page 56)

1) A_r of Ca = 40
   M_r of CaO = (40 + 16) = 56
   mass of Ca = (40 ÷ 56) × 30 = 21.4
   So 21.4 g of Ca reacts.

Revision Summary for Module C6 (page 64)

12) A_r of Mg = 24
    M_r of MgO = (24 + 16) = 40
    mass of MgO = (40 ÷ 24) × 108 = 180
    So 180 g of MgO is produced.

13) (47 ÷ 50) × 100 = 94%

Work (page 72)

Work done = force × distance
Work done = 350 N × 3 m
Work done = 1050 J

Revision Summary for Module P4 (page 75)

1) Speed = distance ÷ time
   Speed = 3.5 m ÷ 35 s = 0.1 m/s

2) Speed = distance ÷ time
   Speed = 6.3 m ÷ 0.5 s = 12.6 m/s
   This is less than 13.3 m/s so no, the car wasn't breaking the speed limit.

11) Momentum = mass × velocity
    Momentum = 78 kg × 5 m/s = 390 kg m/s

14) Work done = force × distance
    Work done = 535 N × 12 m = 6420 J

16) G.P.E. = weight × height
    G.P.E. = 120 N × 4.5 m = 540 J

17) K.E. gained = G.P.E. lost
    K.E. gained = 150 kJ

Revision Summary for Module P5 (page 87)

8) Power = voltage × current
   Power = 230 V × 5 A = 1150 W

11) Resistance = voltage ÷ current
    Resistance = 12 V ÷ 2.5 A = 4.8 Ω